His Messenger

Just as Ellen turned her head, the girl threw a stone that struck her full in the face.

His Messenger

By Ruth Wheeler

Illustrated by Harry Baerg

Pacific Press® Publishing Association
Nampa, Idaho
Oshawa, Ontario, Canada
www.pacificpress.com

Edited by B. Russell Holt
Cover design by Dennis Ferree
Cover Art by Harry Anderson

Revised edition
Copyright © 2001 by
Pacific Press® Publishing Association
Printed in the United States of America
All Rights Reserved

Copyright © 1939 by
Review and Herald® Publishing Association

Additional copies of this book may be purchased at
http://www.adventistbookcenter.com

02 03 04 05 06 • 5 4 3 2 1

Dedicated to

Mary C. McReynolds, M.D.

Whose loving portrayal of the gift of prophecy has inspired hundreds of her students to a new faith in the messenger of God and a new understanding of the message.

CONTENTS

ABOUT THIS BOOK	7
THIS STORY OF A FAITHFUL MESSENGER	8
A BRAVE LITTLE GIRL	9
A BEAUTIFUL DREAM	13
READY TO DO HIS WILL	20
DISAPPOINTED	24
THE ANGEL BRINGS A MESSAGE FROM GOD	29
ELLEN BEARS HIS MESSAGE	35
AND GOD SENT HIS ANGEL	41
HE OPENS THE WAY	45
THE SEVENTH DAY IS THE SABBATH	51
A NEW HOME	56
A WILD COLT TAMED	59
WHEN GOD SPEAKS	67
CARRYING THE MESSAGE	73
CHARLIE TAKES THEM THROUGH	83
THE ANGEL SAID, "WRITE"	89
AN ANGEL UNCOUPLES THE TRAIN	97
A CHILD IS LOST	101
ACROSS THE MISSISSIPPI	104
LETTERS TO THE BOYS	111
THE NARROW WAY	117
A CHRISTMAS LONG TO BE REMEMBERED	122
A STRANGER COMES TO TOWN	129
THE LITTLE LIGHTS OF GOD	133
AN ANGEL POINTS THE WAY	137
THROUGH THE GOLDEN GATE	145
OVERSEAS	149
STRENGTHENED BY HIS PRESENCE	155
PIONEERING IN A FARAWAY LAND	160
A MESSAGE TO A GIRL	169
THE MESSAGE THAT WILL NOT DIE	175
STUDIES FROM THE WRITINGS OF ELLEN G. WHITE	182

About This Book

IN NEARLY every Adventist home there are a number of the wonderful books written by Ellen G. White. While these are read by the older members of the family, the boys and girls have not always realized that many of the truths in these books are for them too. It is to help them to become acquainted with the writer of these precious messages and with the messages themselves that this story of the gift of prophecy has been written.

In Bible times God spoke to His people through His messengers, who were generally called prophets. Through the wisdom and counsel that God gave them, they were able to guide the people. As long as the nation of Israel followed the counsels of the prophets, it prospered and was respected by other nations.

Because of the importance of the times just before the second coming of Jesus, God again chose someone to speak for Him. Mrs. White was only seventeen years old when she began her work, and for seventy years she faithfully bore the messages of God to the church.

The stories in this volume are all true and are taken from Mrs. White's books, letters, and articles printed in various periodicals. Not only are the stories true, but in many cases we have used the very words that Mrs. White used in speaking and writing. In a few places where she wrote *about* what someone said, we have put in the words just as we think he have spoken them. A few times where words have been used by Mrs. White that would not be understood by boys and girls, easier words have been put in their place. We have been very careful, however, not to change in any way the thought she presented.

The books, papers, and letters of Mrs. White are kept in the office of The Ellen G. White Publications at the General Conference headquarters at Washington, D.C. The Board of Trustees who care for these writings are pleased that this book telling of how God used Mrs. White as His messenger has been written. They have allowed me to use letters and other material containing interesting stories for young people. Those in charge of that office have carefully read the manuscript for this book, and they have given their approval to the methods used in presenting this story to our boys and girls.

May you find in this story of the gift of prophecy a new inspiration to study the messages that God has sent to us through His messenger.

RUTH WHEELER

This Story of a Faithful Messenger

When the writer of this book showed me the first part of what she was writing, I said to myself, This is a book the children will read over and over and over again. It was left for a teacher of children to think of writing it, and I think the author has been helped to do the work right. It is a good story also for us who are old.

When I was a child I used to listen, wide awake, when Mrs. White was speaking. She had such a nice, clear, motherly way of telling things that we children could understand even when she was speaking to all the people. And Mrs. White always had a thought for the children.

One of the first books I ever had was a little volume, *Child's Poems,* that Mrs. White selected for children. Then as I grew older I read with interest her books that told of the wonderful things God had shown her to tell to others.

Now I am glad Mrs. Ruth Wheeler has written for the juniors this book of stories about Ellen G. White's life and work in the cause of God. In early youth Mrs. White was called to a special work, and she was faithful and true to the call.

W. A. Spicer

A Brave Little Girl

MORE than a hundred years ago twin girls walked hand in hand across the common, or public park, of Portland, Maine. With them was a schoolmate, and the three friends skipped happily across the grass. Suddenly they heard a shout, and looking back, they saw a girl of about thirteen running after them and calling in an angry voice.

"What's the matter with her?" asked one of the girls.

"I don't know," answered Elizabeth, one of the twins. "But let's run. Mother says not to answer back when someone is angry, but to hurry home."

The three girls started to run as fast as they could, their feet fairly flying over the ground. They were almost across the common when the girl shouted again, and Ellen, Elizabeth's twin sister, looked back to see how close the older girl had come. Just as she was turning her head, the girl threw a stone which she had in her hand.

"Oh," cried Ellen, as the stone struck her full in the face. She was so badly hurt that she sank to the ground. The angry girl, horrified at what she had done, turned and ran away.

The next thing Ellen knew, she was in a store and people were standing about wondering what to do. A kind man stepped forward.

"I will take you home in my carriage," he offered.

His Messenger

"Oh, no! Thank you," Ellen murmured weakly, as she sat up. "I feel stronger now. I can walk. I am afraid the blood will stain your carriage." The people who were in the store did not know how badly the brave little girl was hurt, and so they let her start home, with her sister holding one arm and her schoolmate the other. After she had walked only a short distance she grew faint, and the two girls had to carry her home.

For three weeks Ellen lay in her bed, too sick even to know what was happening or that time was passing. Many of those who saw her felt that she would not live. Ellen's mother prayed earnestly to God for her daughter's life, and He impressed her with the feeling that her little daughter would not die.

When Ellen finally began to notice those about her, she thought she had been asleep. She did not remember the terrible accident.

As she became stronger, neighbors came in to visit and to bring her fruit and flowers.

"What a pity!" said one woman as she left.

"I would not have known her," said another. Ellen wondered what the women could mean.

"Why are they so sorry for me?" she thought. "Do I look different for some reason?" She called for a looking glass. When she saw herself in the mirror she was shocked. Every feature of her face seemed changed. This could not be the round, healthy, smiling face she had always seen reflected in the glass. Then Ellen's mother explained to her that her nose had been broken, and this, with her long illness, had changed her appearance.

"Why do you not prosecute the girl who has ruined Ellen's life?" advised many who came to the house.

"No," answered the mother, who was a faithful Christian

woman. "If it would bring back health to Ellen, there would be something gained, but it would not do that. It would only make enemies."

Ellen felt so sad when she looked at her face in the glass that she almost wished she could die. She was very unhappy. Then the thought came to her that perhaps she might die, and she was frightened, for she felt that she was not ready to die. Her parents had taught their children to trust in the Lord and to turn to Him in prayer. Now Ellen prayed to the Lord that if she was going to die, He would forgive her sins and make her ready to meet Him.

After Ellen had prayed, she felt happy. She loved everyone, even the girl who had struck her. She only wished that all could have their sins forgiven and could love Jesus as she did.

Ellen gained strength very slowly, but at last she was able to join her playmates. She learned then the bitter lesson that one's appearance may make a difference in the treatment one receives. Those who had been happy to have her as their playmate when she was a healthy, lively girl had little sympathy for her now that she was weak and sick and her beauty and health had been destroyed. Ellen felt this deeply, and it made her very unhappy.

When Ellen was hurt, her father, Mr. Harmon, was away on a trip. It was several months before he came home, and he was eager to see his children again. When he came into the house he hugged Ellen's brother and her sisters, and then he looked about for her. She timidly stood back away from the others.

"Where is Ellen?" he asked.

"There she is," said the mother, pointing to where she stood by herself. He looked at Ellen and then back to his wife, thinking, "Surely this is not my little Ellen." It seemed to

His Messenger

him that the pale, thin little girl with the disfigured face, who stood so quietly by herself, could not be his once-happy, healthy daughter. Although she smiled at her father when he took her in his arms, she felt that her heart would break at the thought that not even her own father could recognize her.

At last it was thought that Ellen was strong enough to go to school again. But when she tried to write, her hand trembled so, that she could write only the simplest of words. It seemed impossible for her to study and remember what she had learned.

The teacher asked the girl who had thrown the stone at Ellen while she was crossing the common, to be monitor. It was her duty to help Ellen with her writing and her other lessons. Ellen never reminded her of the accident, but she seemed very sad when she saw Ellen struggling to write her lessons. She was sincerely sorry for her hasty act and for the results of her anger. She was always tender and patient with the poor little pupil.

After a few months the teacher felt that until Ellen should become stronger she should not be allowed to exert herself in school. So she had to give up her studies. It was a severe trial to the little girl to leave school, for she loved her schoolwork and wanted to have a good education.

A Beautiful Dream

"WILLIAM MILLER is preaching tonight," said Ellen's father one day, as he sat down to dinner, "and we must go to hear him. He is preaching a new and strange doctrine. He thinks that Jesus Himself will soon come to this earth. I want to know whether this is from the Bible."

That night the Harmon family went to the meeting held by William Miller in the town of Portland, Maine. How stirred they were as the minister told them of the nearness of the coming of Jesus. Mr. Miller made the explanation from the prophecies so clear that although Ellen was only twelve years old even she could understand it.

This minister was a careful student of the Bible. He found that the prophecies in the book of Daniel concerning the different kingdoms had all come true. Then he came to a prophecy which said that at the end of a period of 2300 years the sanctuary would be cleansed.

"Can we tell when these years will begin and end?" he wondered. He found the answer in the book of Daniel, the ninth chapter. Here he found that this period began when the decree was given to restore and build Jerusalem. From history he learned that this decree was given 457 years before Christ.

The other prophecies in this same chapter concerning the work of Christ and His death, had been fulfilled in the exact year it was prophesied that they should be; so Mr. Miller was confident that the next event, the cleansing of the sanctuary, would take place at the end of the 2300 years. The end of the prophecy would come in 1843.

What was meant by the cleansing of the sanctuary? Bible students know now that the sanctuary here spoken of is in heaven, where Jesus pleads with His Father for the forgiveness of our sins. But at that time nearly all Christians believed that the earth was the sanctuary. Mr. Miller felt sure that the cleansing of the sanctuary meant the cleansing of the earth from sin at the coming of Jesus.

What a thrilling thought this was. Jesus was coming in 1843! He felt that he must tell others about it; so he left his home and went out to preach wherever he could find those who would listen to him. Now he had come to Portland, and was telling the people there why he believed that Jesus would come in only three more years.

Everyone in the city was talking of this great event. Many scoffed and laughed, but scores of others believed. Ellen went to these meetings, and when Mr. Miller asked those who wanted especially to seek God in prayer to come to the front of the hall, she went forward, with many others, and knelt, praying that her sins might be forgiven. Of course Jesus answered her prayer, but she did not feel that He had. She had not yet learned that we must trust Jesus to pardon our sins when we confess them and ask Him to forgive them. For the next few weeks she was troubled, for she was not sure that she was ready to meet Jesus.

The following summer the Harmon family went to the Methodist camp meeting. Ellen was glad to have this opportunity to hear more about Jesus. She went fully resolved to seek the Lord in earnest there, and to be prepared for His coming.

A Beautiful Dream

Soon after they reached the campground, she heard a sermon preached from the words of Queen Esther, "So will I go in unto the king, ... and if I perish, I perish" (Esther 4:16). The sermon was especially for those who were longing to be saved yet were afraid they could not make themselves worthy of the love of God. The words of the minister helped Ellen to understand what she must do to be ready to meet her Saviour when He should come. She understood that she could not through her own strength make herself worthy, but that Jesus alone could cleanse from sin.

Soon after this, as she prayed, her heart was filled with happiness and she now felt that Jesus had forgiven her sins. She realized that Jesus was very near to His children, that they could go to Him with their troubles, and that He would take away all sadness, the same as He had blessed and healed those who came to Him when He was here on this earth.

One of the women spoke to her, "Dear child, have you found Jesus?" As Ellen turned to say Yes, the woman exclaimed, "Indeed, you have. His peace is with you. I see it in your face."

About this time Ellen passed by a tent on the campground and saw a little girl who seemed much distressed about something. She held in her arms a little parasol. Her face was pale as she tightly clung to her treasure. Several times she started to lay it down and then she held it closer to her again. After a few minutes the child cried, "Dear Jesus, I want to love You and go to heaven! Take away my sins! I give myself to You, parasol and all." Then crying, she threw herself into her mother's arms. "Mother," she said, "I am so happy, for Jesus loves me, and I love Him better than my parasol or anything else."

Her face was shining with happiness as she smiled at those about her. Then her mother, with tears in her eyes, ex-

His Messenger

plained that her little daughter had received the parasol as a present not long before. She loved it very much. She carried it with her everywhere, even taking it with her when she went to sleep at night. But during the meetings the little girl had heard that we must give all to Jesus. The little parasol was the dearest thing on earth to her, and so she had felt that she must give it to Jesus. What a struggle she had gone through before she was willing to give up her treasure! But now that it was over, and she had given all she had, her face was bright with her new joy.

Then it was explained to the little girl that since she had given up everything to her Saviour, and allowed nothing to stand between her and her love for Him it was right for her to keep the parasol and use it.

As Ellen walked on across the campground she said to herself, "How hard it is to give up the parasol! Yet Jesus gave up heaven for our sake, and became poor, that we, through His poverty and suffering, might have heavenly riches."

Shortly after her return from camp meeting, she asked to be baptized and taken into the Methodist Church, to which her parents belonged. The leaders in the church urged her to be sprinkled, but she felt that she wanted to be baptized as her Saviour had been, by immersion.

Although the day appointed for the baptism was a windy one, and the waves of the ocean dashed upon the shore, Ellen's heart was happy—happy that she could take up her cross for the Master. Her peace was like a river. She was beginning a new life that was to be a life of service for her Saviour.

Although Ellen became a member of the church and attended the meetings regularly, including the prayer meeting, she had never prayed aloud in public. Now it became impressed upon her mind that she should seek God in prayer in the small prayer meetings. She was very timid, and felt that

A Beautiful Dream

she could not do this, but whenever she knelt alone to pray, this duty came to her mind.

Then one night she had a dream. She dreamed that she was sitting, sadly thinking, with her face in her hands. "If Jesus were upon earth," she thought to herself, "I would go to Him, throw myself at His feet, and tell Him all my sufferings. He would not turn away from me; He would have mercy upon me, and I would love and serve Him always."

While she was thinking, the door opened, and a beautiful person came in. He looked at her kindly and said, "Do you wish to see Jesus? He is here, and you can see Him if you desire. Take everything you possess, and follow me."

She gathered up her little possessions and joyfully followed her guide. He led her to a steep, narrow stairway. As they began to climb the stairs, he warned her to keep looking upward, lest she become dizzy and fall. She saw others climbing the stairs also, who looked down and fell before they reached the top.

Finally Ellen and her guide reached the last step. They stood before a closed door. Her guide told her to leave everything she was carrying. She cheerfully laid her possessions down.

Then he opened the door and told her to go in. In a moment she stood before Jesus. As He looked upon her, she knew that He was acquainted with her and with all her thoughts.

She tried to shield herself from His gaze, but He drew near and laid His hand upon her head. "Fear not," He said, as He smiled upon her. The sound of His sweet voice filled her heart with happiness. She was overcome with joy and sank to the floor at His feet.

Ellen felt, in her dream, that she had reached the peace of heaven. When at last she rose, the loving eyes of Jesus were

Ellen felt in her dream that she had reached the peace of heaven.

A Beautiful Dream

upon her, and His beautiful smile filled her soul with gladness. She looked at Him with holy reverence and love.

Her guide opened the door and they went out. He told her to take up again the possessions she had laid down. Then he handed her a green cord tightly coiled. He told her to place it next to her heart, and when she wanted to see Jesus to take the cord out and stretch it as far as she could. "Do not let it remain coiled very long at a time," the angel said, "or it will become knotted and hard to straighten."

Ellen placed the cord next to her heart and joyfully began her journey back down the narrow stairs. As she went she praised the Lord and told everyone she met where he could find Jesus.

When Ellen awakened she was happy. This dream gave her hope that she could go to God in prayer whenever she desired. To her, the green cord represented faith in God, and she understood how simple it was to trust in Him. She was sure now, that Jesus loved her.

Ready to Do His Will

"Mother," said Ellen one morning, "I had a most beautiful dream last night, and I thought that I saw Jesus. An angel took me to see Him, and He smiled at me."

Then Ellen told her mother all about this dream that had given her comfort and helped her to realize that Jesus loved her and would help her to be prepared to meet Him when He should come to this earth.

Her mother listened tenderly to her daughter.

"Let us go and talk with Mr. Stockman," suggested Mrs. Harmon. "I am sure he would be glad to talk with us."

Together they went to see the minister. When Ellen had told him of her experience, Mr. Stockman laid his hand upon her head, and said, "Ellen, you are only a child. Yours is a singular experience for one of your tender age. Jesus must be preparing you for some special work."

Then with tears in his eyes he told her of the love of God for His sinful children, and of His longing to draw them to Himself in simple faith and trust. He told her that the fear that she was not worthy of heaven was the tender influence of God calling to her. "When a person feels that he is all right, and need not strive to be better, then he is in the greatest danger of losing his hold on God," the minister told her.

"Go free, Ellen," he said; "return to your home trusting in

Ready to Do His Will

Jesus, for He will not withhold His love from any true seeker."

They had prayer together, and the minister asked God's blessing on the young girl. When Ellen and her mother went home, they felt that they had learned a great deal of the love and tenderness of God from this faithful servant of His. Ellen felt that she loved her Saviour enough now to do anything He wanted her to do.

When she knelt to pray by herself, she again felt that God wanted her to pray in public. Ellen resolved that she would pray aloud the next opportunity that came. She did not have long to wait, for there was to be a prayer meeting that night at the home of her uncle.

At the meeting Ellen knelt with the others. She waited, trembling, while several prayed, and then she began to pray. As she praised God, her heart was filled with love and happiness, and everything seemed shut out but Jesus and His glory.

"I have done what God wanted me to do," Ellen said to herself when she started home. How very dear Jesus was to her now! She loved Him as a kind and tender parent, and obedience to His will was a joy. Again and again the young girl softly repeated the words, "The Lord is my shepherd; I shall not want."

The Adventists—that is, those who believed that Jesus was soon coming—held meetings almost every day at homes in different parts of the city in which the Harmon family lived. They still believed, as William Miller had taught them, that Jesus was coming in the year 1843, or at the latest sometime before March 21, 1844. The Harmon family attended the meetings regularly, for they too believed that their Saviour was coming soon. The time seemed so short in which to prepare to meet Jesus that the whole family felt they should do all they could to tell others of their hope. But what could

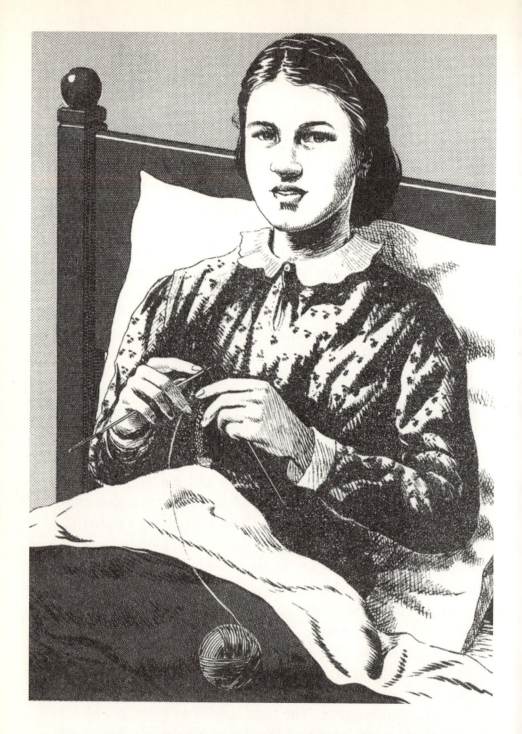
Ellen's heart was very weak, and it was necessary for her to sit propped up in bed to do the knitting.

the children do? The twin girls, Elizabeth and Ellen, and Sarah, who was older, talked the matter over and decided to earn money to buy books and papers telling of Jesus' soon coming, which they could give to their friends.

Mr. Harmon made hats, and the girls were allowed to make the crowns of the hats. Ellen also knitted stockings, which were sold for twenty-five cents a pair. Her heart was very weak at this time, and it was necessary for her to sit propped up in bed to do her work. But she worked on, earning about twenty-five cents a day, happy that her trembling fingers could do something for the cause of God. This money was carefully put away for use in the purchase of books and tracts. Every leaf of this printed matter that the girls bought was very precious in their eyes, for it was a messenger of light, warning people to prepare for the soon coming of the Saviour.

When Ellen became a little stronger, special meetings were arranged in which the young people of the neighborhood could gather together to study God's Word and to pray. Some of these young friends were thoughtless and had very little interest in religion, but night after night Ellen prayed for her friends.

During the day, when opportunity offered, she talked with each one alone, and the result was that every one of these young friends was converted to God. Some of the older Christians felt that Ellen was too eager to tell of the love of her Saviour. When they came to her and complained, the earnest little Christian told them that she could not stop telling of the love of God when His coming was so near, and that God Himself was leading her in this work.

"I feel like a little child coming to God as to my father, and asking Him what He would have me to do," she said. "Then as my duty is made plain to me, it is my greatest happiness to do it."

Disappointed

As THE time set for the coming of Jesus drew near, how earnest His followers became! With what carefulness and trembling they approached the time when the Saviour was to appear! The affairs of this world did not interest them, for they expected in just a few short months to be going home. Meetings were held in churches and in private homes.

In the city of Portland, Maine, the large Beethoven Hall was crowded nightly as the rich and the poor, the ministers and their followers, and all classes of people came to the hall to hear the Advent message as it was presented by Mr. Stockman, who for some time had been preaching there. There was almost perfect stillness in the great hall as he spoke of his desire to welcome his Saviour when He should come in the clouds. There was a solemn, searching power in his words.

The order of the meetings was simple. He preached a short sermon, and then a general discussion was entered into, with questions asked and answered. There was never any argument, for the presence of the holy angels was too greatly felt as the people earnestly sought for the truth.

At the close of the meetings those who desired the prayers of the people of God were asked to rise. Sometimes hundreds rose and earnestly asked to be remembered in prayer.

After the meetings closed, the people would return to

Disappointed

their homes through the darkness. As they walked along, a voice praising God would come drifting across the fields, and then an answer would be called back from another road, "Glory to God, the Lord reigneth!" Another and another would take up the call. Families would go to their homes with songs upon their lips, as the praises rang out through the still night air. No one who attended those meetings could ever forget the solemn scenes.

Finally came the last weeks of the time the believers expected to spend on this earth. The people were filled with great earnestness. Worldly business was laid aside while they carefully searched their hearts to make sure that they were ready to meet their Lord. But the time passed, and Jesus did not come. There had been some mistake.

This was the first real test brought to those who expected the Lord to come at that time. Those who did not believe made fun of the waiting ones, and scoffed at them. Many had joined the company of waiting believers because they feared that the Lord might come, not because they loved Him and longed for His appearing. These at once joined the scoffers and said that they never had really believed anyway.

The true believers knew that the word of the Lord was sure and would not fail. They had done their duty, and now they waited with hope and trust that God would make all things clear to them.

In the summer of 1844 many of the Adventists were gathered in a large camp meeting. Here they studied together again the Bible truths, to find every bit of light they could about the near coming of Jesus. As they studied into the matter more fully they found that the decree was given near the end of the year 457, and this would bring the time of His coming later in 1844.

"The prophecy of the 2300 days says that at the end of

His Messenger

that time the sanctuary will be cleansed," said one of the leaders. "By a study of the services in the sanctuary used by the Israelites, we find that the cleansing of the sanctuary took place on the Day of Atonement."

"When is the Day of Atonement?" one of his listeners eagerly asked.

"The tenth day of the seventh month of the Jewish year," he answered.

"And what day of our year is that?"

"It will be October 22."

"Jesus will come on that day," they agreed. Again their hearts were thrilled with happiness. Soon they would see their Lord coming. The message was passed on to others. The hopes of the Advent people were now centered on the coming of the Lord on October 22, 1844. They read again the story of the ten virgins and the marriage party that was delayed until midnight, when the cry went forth, "Behold, the bridegroom cometh; go ye out to meet him."

"We are in the time before midnight when the bridegroom was delayed," one believer said. "It is almost time for Him to come."

"We have all been asleep," one said to another. "We must awaken and go out to meet our Lord."

As this midnight cry spread, the whole nation was stirred. A paper called the *Midnight Cry* was published and scattered everywhere. Thousands sought out the little companies of Advent believers to learn more of this message. Many sold their property and gave their money to the workers to help scatter the *Midnight Cry,* the *Signs of the Times,* and other papers with the same important message.

Many of the Adventists left their crops in the fields unharvested, for what need had they of winter supplies? A brother in New Hampshire had a large field of potatoes,

People laughed at the disappointed believers who had taught that Jesus would come to this earth in 1844.

which he left undug. His anxious neighbors offered to dig them free and put them in his cellar.

"No," said the brother, "I am going to let that field of potatoes preach my faith in the Lord's soon appearing."

With happy hearts the waiting people of God confidently approached the hour when they expected their Lord to return. On October 22 they gathered in little companies, praying and singing hymns together while they watched for His appearing.

But that night the sun set as usual without the great event's taking place. Jesus had not come.

It was a bitter disappointment to these faithful ones whose courage had been so strong. It was hard to take up again the duties of this life which they had thought to lay down forever. But the love of God sustained them in this trial, and they were surprised that they felt so courageous and were able to meet with such strength the taunts of their enemies.

The believers did not complain at the trials that had come to them, but waited patiently for the Saviour to make known His will. Some felt that they must be mistaken in the *event* to take place at the end of the 2300 years, and not in the calculation of the time. They realized that the preaching of the definite time had been guided by God, for it had led the whole nation to awaken to the need for study of the Bible, and had led many to become acquainted with their Saviour.

The Angel Brings a Message From God

It is always hard to be disappointed, and it is hard to go back to what we have cast aside forever. How the hearts of the faithful believers ached as they realized that the Lord had not come at the time they had expected Him.

Nothing had stood between them and their preparation for the great day. No provision had been made for "if the Lord doesn't come." But the faithful ones did not fear. They rejoiced that they had acted according to their faith. They must look to God to lead them, and they knew that He would have a plan for their future.

Early the next morning after the Disappointment, Hiram Edson, a leader among the Adventists in western New York, went out into the field and knelt down to pray beside a shock of corn. He felt that the Lord was near him as he prayed. Suddenly the presence of the Lord became so real that he was almost overcome, and a voice seemed to speak to him, saying, "The sanctuary to be cleansed is in heaven." He hurried to tell some of his brethren of his conviction, and they began with him to study the subject from the Bible.

This new interpretation of the event to take place on the day of the Disappointment brought courage to many when they heard it. It was then clear to them that they had misunderstood what was to happen at the end of the 2300 days. Many

The man in New Hampshire found that his crop of potatoes had been saved because he had not dug them at the regular time.

The Angel Brings a Message From God

others felt that they must have been mistaken in the exact time when the 2300 days should end.

After the Disappointment the believers had to prepare for winter, but none were left in want. The man in New Hampshire who would not allow his neighbors to dig his potatoes, because he wished his unharvested crop to preach his faith in the second coming of Christ, was rewarded. That fall a potato rot destroyed the crops throughout New England. But the autumn was mild, and the potatoes that had been left in the ground did not freeze, and neither did they rot. The faithful man had an abundant supply for himself and for his neighbors. Others throughout the country had much the same experience.

The people needed the presence of their Saviour with them at this time more than they ever had before, and He did not disappoint them. He chose to use a very special gift for the encouragement of the people—the gift of prophecy. Since Creation He had spoken to His children through this gift when they especially needed His help.

Ellen Harmon, who had served the Lord with all her heart since she was a child, was chosen by the heavenly Father as His messenger. Within two months after this disappointment He spoke to her and gave her messages for the believers.

Ellen was only seventeen years old at this time. She was still in very poor health, and her throat and lungs were so diseased that she could scarcely speak above a whisper. The doctors said that she might live only a short time. One morning at worship she was kneeling in prayer with four other women. All the others had prayed, and Ellen was praying in a whisper when the power of God was felt by all present. In a moment Ellen ceased praying and remained silent. She was hearing the voice of the angel of God as he spoke to her. It seemed to her that she was surrounded by a light and was rising higher and higher from the earth. She turned to look for the Advent people in the world, but she could not find them. Then a voice said, "Look a little higher." When she looked up she saw a straight, narrow path high above the world, leading to the heavenly city beyond. On this path the Advent people were traveling. A light set up at the beginning of the path shone all along the way, lighting the feet of the travelers so that they would not stumble. "This light," said the angel, "is the midnight cry."

In the front of the company, leading them to the city, was Jesus. As long as His followers kept their eyes fixed upon Him, they were safe, but some grew tired, and complained that the city was a great way off. Then Jesus raised His right arm, and from it a light shone back all along the path, and the little band of followers shouted with joy. But some lost sight of Jesus, and said that it was not God who had led them. The light behind them went out, and they were left in complete darkness. They stumbled in the dark and fell from the path down into the world below.

Soon the company who were following Jesus heard the voice of God, which told them the day and hour of Jesus' coming. They knew and understood the voice, but the people in the world below thought it was thunder and an earthquake. The faces of the little band of followers were lighted up by the glory of God and shone as did the face of Moses when he came down from Sinai after speaking there with God.

Ellen Harmon was then shown the coming of the Saviour in the clouds of heaven. She heard the group of believers cry out, "Who shall be able to stand?" There was an awful silence. Then the voice of Jesus spoke, "Those who have clean hands and pure hearts shall be able to stand: My grace is sufficient for you." At this, joy filled every heart. The angels' songs rang through the air. She saw the dead raised from their graves, and

The Angel Brings a Message From God

saw their loved ones greet them with shouts of joy. Then those who were ready to meet the Lord were taken with Him into the cloud. When the company had reached the city of gold, she saw Jesus lay hold of the gate of pearl and swing it back on its glittering hinges, saying, "You who have washed your robes in My blood and stood stiffly for My truth, enter in."

After the vision was ended, Ellen realized that she was still kneeling in the parlor of the little home in South Portland, Maine. But how dark this world seemed to her! She had seen a better land.

When Ellen told the members of the Portland church what God had shown her, she said, "While under the power of the Lord, I was filled with joy. I seemed to be surrounded by holy angels in the glorious courts of heaven, where all is peace and gladness."

The members of the church all believed that God had chosen this way to comfort and strengthen His people after the great disappointment they had suffered. How happy they all were to know that their heavenly Father was watching over and caring for them.

An unspeakable awe filled Ellen that she, so young and feeble, should be chosen as the instrument by which God would give light to His people.

While Ellen was praying, it seemed to her that a ball of fire fell on her, and she seemed to be in the presence of the angels.

Ellen Bears His Message

ABOUT a week after the angel of the Lord first spoke to Ellen Harmon in a vision, he appeared to her a second time. He told her that she must make known to others what had been shown her. She was shown the trials she must pass through in her work, and was told that some people would not believe her, but would try to keep her from giving the messages of God. But the angel added, "The grace of God is sufficient for you; He will sustain you."

She was much troubled when she realized what God wanted her to do. She was only seventeen years old, small, frail, and timid, and so retiring that she always avoided meeting strangers if possible. How could she, a young girl, travel from place to place, telling what God had shown her?

For several days she prayed that the responsibility might be taken from her and laid on someone else more capable of bearing it. But the words of the angel, "Make known to others what I have revealed to you," kept ringing in her ears.

"Father," said Ellen one day, "if only you could go with me, I would not fear to go, but I cannot go alone. You have your business to attend to, and what shall I do?"

"Do not worry, my child," he gently answered, "if God has called you to labor in other places He will not fail to open the way for you."

His Messenger

Not long after this a meeting was called at the Harmon home. Ellen was there, and her father told these faithful friends of the struggle she was having. They all united in praying for the young girl, while she herself prayed. Again Ellen felt willing to make every sacrifice necessary to do the work God had for her.

While she was praying, the troubled feeling left, and her heart was filled with praise to God. Suddenly it appeared to Ellen that a bright light like a ball of fire fell upon her. She seemed to be in the presence of the angels. Again the angel spoke and said, "Make known to others what has been revealed to you."

An elderly man, whom the believers called Father Pearson, met with the little company, but he did not have full confidence in the message that had been given to Ellen during her first vision.

Because he had rheumatism he could not kneel during the prayer and sat facing the kneeling group. When the prayer was finished and the company were seated, the old man said, "I have seen a sight such as I never expected to see. A ball of fire came down from heaven and struck Sister Ellen Harmon right on the heart. *I saw it! I saw it!* I can never forget it. It has changed my whole being. Sister Ellen, have courage in the Lord. After this night I will never doubt again. We will help you henceforth, and not discourage you."

Ellen was willing to bear the messages of God, but she was afraid that she might become proud because of the gift that God had given her. She pleaded with the angel that she might be kept from being exalted.

"Your prayers are heard, and shall be answered," the angel told her. "Deliver the message faithfully; endure unto the end, and you shall eat the fruit of the tree of life and drink of the water of life."

Ellen Bears His Message

What a beautiful promise this was! Ellen gave herself to the Lord, ready to do His will, whatever that might be.

She had an opportunity to obey God within only a few days. Unexpectedly, her brother-in-law came from Poland, Maine, thirty miles away, and offered to take her home with him in his sleigh. It was winter, and Ellen was frail, but she decided that this was the way the Lord was calling her to go. With buffalo robes and furs wrapped around her, she started on the cold journey.

From her sister's home she went to a nearby meetinghouse, where the little company of Adventists asked her to tell what God had shown her.

She stood up in meeting and began to speak in a whisper. Because of the throat trouble with which she had been ill, she had not spoken aloud for several months. The people leaned forward to catch each whispered word as she spoke, but in a few minutes her voice came clear and strong. The soreness and obstruction in her throat had left.

She spoke to this discouraged, disappointed little group of people for two hours, and how their hearts must have thrilled as she unfolded before them the glories of heaven as they had been shown to her. When Ellen's message was ended she sat down, and when she turned to speak to someone sitting near, she could speak only in the low, husky tones she had been using for three months. The next time she had opportunity to speak to a group of believers, her voice was restored again. Ellen felt a constant assurance that she was doing the will of God, and great peace filled her heart as she saw the courage that her message brought to the faithful ones who had suffered such disappointment.

As Ellen Harmon spoke in the meetinghouse, a young man named Hazen Foss waited at the door to listen. He would not come in, but he plainly heard her clear, strong voice as she told

His Messenger

of what God had shown her of the journeys of the Advent believers.

The man at the door listened closely to her message. He was greatly disturbed. Turning to one of those who stood beside him, he said, "The vision Ellen is relating is as near like what was shown to me as two persons could relate the same thing."

When Ellen finished speaking, Hazen Foss turned away from the steps of the meetinghouse with a heavy heart. He had rejected God, and the message was not for him. A few months before, while the people were waiting for the Lord to come, God had shown him the same vision. Hazen Foss was a young minister. He was an eloquent speaker, and was well liked by all who knew him. The message "Make known to others what I have revealed to you" was also given to him, but he did not understand the vision, and being of a proud spirit, he refused to tell others what had been shown him. He would not humble himself before the people by telling them the message of God, when he could not explain the meaning. The young minister feared they would not believe him, and this would hurt his influence.

The vision was shown to him a second time, and he was told that if he refused to give the message, the burden would be taken from him and given to one of the weakest of God's children, one who would faithfully relate what God would reveal. But still he stubbornly refused to relate what he did not understand. Soon after this, the angel appeared to him a third time. This time the angel only told him that he was released and that the responsibility would be laid upon the weakest of the weak, one who would do God's bidding.

This startled the young man. At once he decided to obey God's will. He called the people together and told them that he had a message for them from heaven. The people crowded

Ellen Bears His Message

together to hear. But when Mr. Foss tried to relate the vision he could not speak a word. It was too late! He stood before the people dumb.

The morning after Hazen Foss heard Ellen Harmon repeat the same vision that had been taken from him, he met her unexpectedly in the hallway of the house. He spoke to her and said, "Ellen Harmon, I heard you talk last night. I believe the visions are taken from me and given to you. Be faithful in bearing the burden and in relating the testimonies of the Lord, and you will not be forsaken of God. I am a lost man. You are chosen of God. Be faithful in doing your work, and the crown I might have had you will receive."

It was immediately after his decision that he would not deliver the message that the first vision was given to Ellen Harmon. Now Mr. Foss had lost his hope in God and was in despair. Never again did he meet with the believers.

Samuel came to Eli in bed, because he thought he had called him.

And God Sent His Angel

THE angel who spoke to Ellen Harmon in vision has carried God's messages to this earth for thousands of years. We might call him the angel of prophecy, for he is the angel who spoke to the prophets whose revelations of the divine will are recorded in the Bible.

In the beginning God walked with Adam in the Garden and talked with him face to face. But Adam sinned. For his disobedience he lost his home in the Garden. He also lost what was far more valuable and sacred to him—the privilege of speaking face to face with his Creator.

But the Master did not forsake Adam when he sinned and was cast out of the Garden. He sent His comforting words to him by an angel messenger. This angel flew swiftly to man, and brought to him the counsel and comfort that God had sent.

After many years there were whole tribes of people living on the earth. Many times the heavenly Father sent His messenger angel to those who would listen to His words.

The persons to whom God sent this special messenger were called prophets. God said, "Hear now my words: If there be a prophet among you, I the Lord will make myself known unto him in a vision, and will speak unto him in a dream" (Num. 12:6). The messages that God gave to the prophets were to be held sacred by the people, for were they not the words of God?

We have record in the Bible of the messages of God that were given to these prophets. Many times God sent His angel to Abraham to tell him what was going to happen, and to guide him in his work. And before the time of Abraham the angel was sent to Enoch and to Noah and to many other prophets.

The little boy Samuel was called by the Lord while he lay in his little bed at night. Three times the Lord called, "Samuel," but the young lad thought it was Eli, the aged priest, calling him. When Eli realized that it was God's voice which had spoken, he reverently told the boy how to answer.

When the voice spoke again, the boy answered, "Speak; for thy servant heareth." Then the message of the Lord was given to the child. When Samuel grew older he became a judge over Israel. Many times the angel of prophecy came to him with messages from the Lord, and all through his long life of service he was ever faithful in delivering these to the people for whom they were sent.

Samuel was known from Dan to Beersheba as "a man of God, ... an honourable man." It is said that none of his words fell to the ground; there were no idle, wasted words in his speech.

Sometimes the Lord showed him things that were to come to pass in the future. The people said of Samuel's messages, "All that he saith cometh surely to pass."

When Daniel was a servant in the courts of Babylon, the angel of prophecy appeared to him. Daniel tells us that this angel's name was Gabriel. The angel showed the prophet the events that would take place down through the ages clear to the end of time.

John the apostle, the beloved of Christ, was sent to the

And God Sent His Angel

island of Patmos as a prisoner. While John was there on that rugged island, Gabriel, the angel of prophecy, came and spoke with him. He opened up before the prophet the glories of heaven. In vision John saw the redeemed of earth, and heard the music of the angels. He was shown scene after scene of thrilling interest in the experiences through which the church would pass before the end of time.

This revelation and other messages to the churches were given to John for the guidance of the Christian church. He was told to write in a book the things he had been shown in vision, that others might read and know the plan that God had for them.

John called the book that he wrote, The Revelation. He said that it was the "Revelation of Jesus Christ, which God gave unto him, to shew unto his servants" the things which would come to pass. Jesus sent this message to John the prophet by His own angel, the messenger angel of prophecy.

Once when Gabriel, the messenger angel, came to John, he showed him in vision the new earth and the tree of life, and the river of life that flows out of the throne of God. He told John that there would be no death in heaven, and no night, for the Lord would give light to the people, and that the redeemed of earth should reign forever and ever. The glories he described as he told of the home we shall have in heaven were almost too wonderful for John to understand or believe.

But the angel told him, "These sayings are faithful and true: and the Lord God of the holy prophets sent his angel to shew unto his servants the things which must shortly be done."

Then the angel added the words of the Master, "Behold, I come quickly: blessed is he that keepeth the sayings of the prophecy of this book."

His Messenger

In telling of the visit of the angel messenger, John writes, "I John saw these things, and heard them. And when I had heard and seen, I fell down to worship before the feet of the angel which shewed me these things."

"See thou do it not," the angel said: "for I am thy fellow-servant, and of thy brethren the prophets, and of them which keep the sayings of this book." And then he added, "Worship God."

The messenger angel who carries the word of God is a servant of God. John also was a servant of God, and he shared with the angel in bearing the message. They were fellow servants. They both bore the testimony of Jesus, the Spirit of prophecy, to the Christian church. The angel Gabriel is a fellow servant of those who keep the sayings of the book of Revelation, which he told John to write. Not until the end of time will the work of Gabriel, the messenger angel, be finished on this earth.

John, on his barren island, was shown a church that would "keep the sayings of this book," and be waiting to welcome Jesus when He comes. He saw that this church would be keeping the commandments of God, and that it would be different from all others because it would have the testimony of Jesus, which is the Spirit of prophecy.

Is it not an inspiring thought that this same angel, who was sent to Daniel, to John, and to the other prophets, to Zacharias, and to Mary, the mother of Jesus, was also sent to Ellen Harmon? This angel said to Zacharias, "I am Gabriel, that stand in the presence of God." How wonderful it is that the angel who stands in the very presence of God is sent to this world with messages to guide and encourage His people!

He Opens the Way

IT WAS a great encouragement to the followers of God after the disappointment of 1844 to have His message sent to them through Ellen Harmon. God in His tender mercy knew how much they needed counsel during this time of discouragement!

Soon after the meeting held near Poland, Maine, the way opened for Miss Harmon to go to the eastern part of the State. A young man and his sister were taking this trip and urged her to go with them. She dreaded going to this new place, but since she had promised the Lord to walk in the path He opened before her she dared not refuse.

After that, as she went to other places, her sister often traveled with her, for she was not strong enough to travel alone. Sometimes one of the brethren and his wife also went with them.

She gave great courage to the believers by her visits. At one place she was given a vision from the Lord, rebuking some of the people of that community because they were not willing to follow the Word of God, but wanted to worship as they pleased. It was especially hard for Ellen Harmon to give this kind of message to these people, but she faithfully delivered the rebuke to them. Of course, it made the ones who insisted on having their own way very angry to have this

Ellen looked out the window to see a man driving up to the gate at a fast pace.

He Opens the Way

young girl point out their sins. They did not realize it was God, not Miss Harmon, who was pointing out these wrongs.

One night while Ellen was in her father's home in Portland, Maine, she was shown that she must go to a town in New Hampshire, called Portsmouth, and bear her testimony to the group of Adventists there. She had no money to pay her fare, but she did not hesitate. The heavenly Father who had sent her the message to go, would provide the way. She and her sister dressed and prepared to go.

She heard the first bell of the train ring. She put on her hat and walked to the window. When she looked out she saw a man, who was driving his horse very fast, hurry up to the gate and stop. His horse was covered with sweat.

"Is there anyone here who needs money?" he called as he ran toward the house. "I was impressed that someone here needed money."

Hastily the sisters explained to him that they had to go to Portsmouth but didn't have the money to pay their fare. The man quickly handed them money enough to pay their fare to Portsmouth and back.

"Take a seat in my wagon, and I will take you to the depot," he said. When the girls were seated, he turned his horse toward the depot.

"I have come twelve miles to bring you this money," he explained. "I could not hold my horse back; he seemed driven to go faster and faster."

They arrived at the station just in time to board the car and find seats before the train started.

This experience gave Ellen much courage. It strengthened her faith to have this proof that God expected her only to do His will and He would open the way.

While attending meetings at New Bedford, Massachusetts, Ellen Harmon met a sea captain, Joseph Bates. He had

His Messenger

accepted the Advent faith about a year before the Harmon family had, and was an active laborer in the cause. Mr. Bates was very happy to meet this young woman of whom he had heard. He was a true gentleman, and treated Ellen as kindly as though she were his own child.

When she talked to the believers soon after she arrived, the captain was deeply interested. After she had finished, he arose and spoke.

"I am a doubting Thomas. I do not believe in visions," he bluntly said. "But if I could believe that the testimony the sister has related tonight was indeed the voice of God to us, I should be the happiest man alive. My heart is moved. I believe the speaker to be sincere, but I cannot explain to my satisfaction her being shown the wonderful things she has related to us."

Captain Bates had followed the sea for twenty-one years, first as a cabin boy, then as a sailor, and later as the master and owner of the ships he sailed. As a navigator he was familiar with the stars and their positions in the sky.

"I can very nearly tell where I am upon the sea, as to latitude and longitude, without using my charts," he often remarked, "just by observing the stars and the sun and moon."

The captain was interested in astronomy, and enjoyed talking to those who were familiar with the stars. At one time he spoke to Miss Harmon and mentioned his interest in the study of the stars, but he soon found that she knew very little about them. She told the captain that she did not believe she had ever even looked into a book that told about the stars.

In the fall of 1846 Ellen was married to James White. Mr. White was a sincere young Christian who was anxious to serve the Lord. Together they traveled and devoted their efforts to the cause of the Advent message. Shortly after their marriage Mr. and Mrs. White went to Topsham, Maine, to

He Opens the Way

attend a conference that was being held there. Captain Bates was also present at this meeting. One evening during the conference, as the workers were in meeting in the home of one of the believers, Ellen White was given a vision. While in vision, in the presence of all, she began to speak of the things the messenger angel was revealing to her. Suddenly she began to talk about the stars and to describe their beauties as she saw them. She told of seeing rosy-tinted belts crossing the surface of one planet.

"I see four moons," said the young woman in vision.

"Oh, she is viewing Jupiter," said Captain Bates, as he leaned forward in breathless interest. Mrs. White continued to describe what she saw, telling of the belts and rings in their ever-changing beauty, and said, "I see seven moons."

"She is describing Saturn," exclaimed the captain.

"I see six moons," continued the girl, as she told of the beauties of another planet.

While she was still talking and in vision, Captain Bates arose and exclaimed, "This is a better description of the heavenly bodies than anything I have ever read on the subject." Then with his face shining with the light of heaven, he added, "This is of the Lord."

Mrs. White knew nothing about astronomy, and did not know the names of the planets and stars she was shown, and the messenger angel did not name them. They may not have been the ones that Captain Bates thought they were, by her description.

Captain Bates was fully satisfied that the vision of the young woman was outside her knowledge, and that it was indeed from the Lord. He praised God, and his smiling face expressed his happiness.

"I believe," he said, "that this vision concerning the planets was given that I might never doubt again."

William Farnsworth and his son Daniel worked by the side of the road the next Sunday, to show that they did not consider the day sacred.

The Seventh Day Is the Sabbath

THE farmers living among the rocky hills near the little village of Washington, New Hampshire, had heard the message that Jesus was soon coming, and were earnest in looking for Him. They had built a little church out in the woods, where they held their meetings.

A young woman, nineteen years old, was hired to teach the country school. Her name was Delight Oakes. When she went to Washington, her mother moved there with her. They were Seventh Day Baptists, and although there was no one else in the village to meet with them, Delight and her mother were faithful in the observance of the seventh day.

The Adventists became acquainted with these new neighbors, and began to talk to them about the coming of Jesus. "He is coming soon," they said, "and we are preparing to meet Him." They read from their Bibles the texts that spoke of His coming again to this earth. Mrs. Oakes and her daughter loved the Bible, and were glad to study with them. After they had talked to Mrs. Oakes about the coming of Christ, she said:

"I want to ask you a question. Why do you not keep the Sabbath of the Lord? Why do you worship Him on Sunday?"

"Why do you ask that?" someone said. "Isn't Sunday the Sabbath of the Lord?"

His Messenger

"Indeed, it is not," said Mrs. Oakes. She opened the Bible and read to them the texts about the seventh-day Sabbath. She knew just what the Lord had said about His holy day.

Mrs. Oakes and her daughter were so certain that the Lord wanted His people to keep the Sabbath that they could not believe He would come to translate His waiting ones until they had turned to keep all the commandments.

The Adventist farmers in Washington were just as certain regarding the coming of the Lord at the end of the 2300 years, in 1844, as their neighbors were regarding the seventh day's being the Sabbath.

After the time passed, some of the farmers began to think more seriously about the Sabbath. They read the tracts that had been given them on the subject. One Sunday, William Farnsworth stood up in the little meetinghouse and said, "Brethren, I am going to keep the Sabbath." There was silence in the church. Many of the other members sat with bowed heads. "I am convinced that the seventh day is the Sabbath of the Lord," he added.

After a few moments another one stood and said, "I too want to obey the Lord's command." Others decided that day to keep God's Sabbath. The next Sabbath, Mrs. Oakes and her daughter and a few other families met at the home of Cyrus Farnsworth to worship God.

The next day, Sunday, William Farnsworth and his son Daniel worked by the side of the road, so that their neighbors who passed on the way to church could see that they no longer considered Sunday the right day to keep holy.

As time went on, others joined the company who worshiped on the seventh day, until nearly all were united, and then they held their meetings in the church. Frederick Wheeler, a minister, united with them, and was their leader. This was the first company of Sabbathkeeping Adventists.

The Seventh Day Is the Sabbath

The next spring, in 1845, Joseph Bates went to visit this small company of Adventists. When he arrived at the little village, the Adventists welcomed him. They gladly answered his questions about the seventh-day Sabbath. Mr. Bates carefully studied the texts they pointed out to him. They then gave him an article written by Mr. Preble, showing how the Sabbath had been changed by men who wished to keep the first day of the week instead of the seventh. Mr. Bates was much interested.

"Surely," he said, "this is the truth. Sabbath is the seventh day. It is the day God set apart at Creation, and He has never changed it. The seventh day is still the Sabbath of the Lord."

Of course, Mr. Bates could not keep this wonderful news to himself. He must go and tell the Adventists in his home town of this wonderful message. He at once set out to return to New Bedford, Massachusetts.

Near New Bedford was a bridge. As the captain started across this bridge, he met a prominent man of the community.

"Captain Bates, what's the news?" he called out as he saw the captain hurrying along.

"The news is that the seventh day is the Sabbath of the Lord," answered Mr. Bates, as he paused to greet his friend.

"Well," said the man, "I will go home and read my Bible and see about that." Mr. Bates hurried on, and the man went back to his home. When next they met, the man was also keeping the seventh-day Sabbath.

Mr. Bates continued telling the people wherever he went that the seventh day was the Sabbath. After a year he wrote a small book telling of the Sabbath truth, and had it sent to those who were interested. This caused many to study, and they too started to worship God on the Sabbath.

While Mr. Bates was writing his book, Ellen Harmon and others visited him in New Bedford. He talked earnestly to them about the wonderful truth he had found in his Bible, that the seventh day is still the Sabbath. But Ellen did not then see the importance of the Sabbath question. She had never particularly studied the matter, and did not think it was very important. She felt that Mr. Bates made a mistake in talking so much about the fourth commandment. Soon after this she was married to James White, and together they studied the book written by Mr. Bates and compared it with the Bible.

As they studied and compared scripture with scripture, they found that the Lord had never given command to change the Sabbath day. They studied history, and found that the day had been changed by men who wished to worship on the first day of the week instead of the seventh.

Soon they became fully convinced that it was the Lord's will, and they too began to keep the seventh-day Sabbath and to teach it. This was in the autumn of the year 1846. How happy Mr. Bates must have been as he saw these earnest workers in the cause of God finding the true Sabbath.

On the first Sabbath in April of the next year Mr. and Mrs. White went to a meeting held at the home of Stockbridge Howland, a devoted Adventist. While they were there, a vision was given to Mrs. White in which she saw the importance of the Sabbath. She saw the temple of God opened in heaven, and she was shown the ark of God, covered with the mercy seat. Two angels stood, one at each end of the ark, with their wings spread over the mercy seat, and their faces turned toward it. The messenger angel told her that these two angels represented the whole host of heavenly angels, who look with reverent awe toward the holy law that was written by the finger of God on the tables of stone. Jesus raised the cover of the ark, and she saw the tables of stone with the Ten Commandments written upon them.

The Seventh Day Is the Sabbath

As she looked she saw that the fourth commandment had a soft halo of light all around it.

"It is the only one of the ten which defines the living God, who created the heavens and the earth and all living things that are therein," said the angel. "When the foundations of the earth were laid, then was also laid the foundation of the Sabbath."

A New Home

THE Adventist believers were anxious to know more of the heavenly kingdom, where they hoped to make their eternal home. The description of the New Jerusalem, as given in the book of Revelation, was read many times, and the faithful ones encouraged one another by recounting the joys of life with Jesus.

In a vision God sent to Ellen G. White, she was shown the beauties of this earth as it will be when the followers of God again live here.

In vision she was taken to heaven. She was shown the company of redeemed people returning to this earth, with Jesus leading them. "With Jesus at our head we all descended from the city down to this earth, on a great and mighty mountain, which could not bear Jesus up, and it parted asunder, and there was a mighty plain," said Mrs. White, as she told the believers what had been shown her. "Then we looked up and saw the great city, with twelve foundations, and twelve gates, three on each side, and an angel at each gate. We all cried out, 'The city, the great city, it's coming, it's coming down from God out of heaven,' and it came and settled on the place where we stood.

"Then we began to look at the glorious things outside of the city. There I saw most glorious houses, that had the appearance of silver, supported by four pillars set with pearls most glorious to behold. These were to be inhabited by the saints. In each was a golden shelf. I saw many of the saints go into the houses, take off their glittering crowns and lay them on the shelf, then go out into the field by the houses to do something with the earth; not as we have to do with the earth here. . . .

"I saw another field full of all kinds of flowers, and as I plucked them, I cried out, 'They will never fade.' Next I saw a field of tall grass, most glorious to behold; it was living green and had a reflection of silver and gold, as it waved proudly to the glory of King Jesus.

"Then we entered a field full of all kinds of beasts—the lion, the lamb, the leopard, and the wolf, all together in perfect union. We passed through the midst of them, and they followed on peaceably after. Then we entered a wood, not like the dark woods we have here; no, no; but light, and all over glorious; the branches of the trees waved to and fro, and we all cried out, 'We will dwell safely in the wilderness and sleep in the woods.' . . .

"As we were traveling along, we met a company who also were gazing at the glories of the place. I noticed red as a border on their garments; their crowns were brilliant; their robes were pure white. As we greeted them, I asked Jesus who they were. He said they were martyrs that had been slain for Him. With them was an innumerable company of little ones; they also had a hem of red on their garments.

"Mount Zion was just before us, and on the mount was a glorious temple, and about it were seven other mountains, on which grew roses and lilies. And I saw the little ones climb, or, if they chose, use their little wings and fly, to the top of the mountains and pluck the never-fading flowers. . . .

"After we beheld the glory of the temple, we went out, and Jesus left us and went to the city. Soon we heard His lovely voice again, saying, 'Come, My people, you have come out of great tribulation, and done My will; suffered for Me; come in to supper, for I will gird Myself, and serve you.'

"We shouted, 'Alleluia! glory!' and entered into the city. And I saw a table of pure silver; it was many miles in length, yet our eyes could extend over it. I saw the fruit of the tree of life, the manna, almonds, figs, pomegranates, grapes, and many other kinds of fruit.

"I asked Jesus to let me eat of the fruit. He said, 'Not now. Those who eat of the fruit of this land go back to earth no more. But in a little while, if faithful, you shall both eat of the fruit of the tree of life and drink of the water of the fountain.' And He said, 'You must go back to the earth again and relate to others what I have revealed to you.'

"Then an angel bore me gently down to this dark world."

The faithful believers felt like shouting "Hallelujah" themselves when they heard this glorious description of the new earth.

"Surely God is good," they told one another, "for He has gone to prepare a place for us, and we shall see Him there."

A Wild Colt Tamed

A WILD colt was feeding in the pasture of one of the Adventist men who lived near Topsham, Maine. This colt belonged to a man who lived many miles away, and he wanted him brought home. He didn't have time to come after the horse, so he suggested that someone coming up that way drive the colt home.

No one wanted to drive the young animal, for he had been mistreated by the men who were trying to train him, and had become badly frightened, until it was almost impossible to manage him. Once when the men were trying to drive him, the colt had become so frightened that he had run against the rocky cliff at the side of the road and crushed one of the men to death.

If someone did hitch up the colt to a buggy, the reins had to be held tightly and not allowed to touch the flanks of the colt, for if anything touched him, he at once began to kick furiously.

Shortly after the meeting at Topsham, Maine, in which Mr. Bates was so happy because he felt that God had sent the vision of the stars especially for him, Mr. and Mrs. White decided to go to the town where the owner of the colt lived.

"Mr. White, why don't you drive that colt back to its owner, since you're going there now?" suggested someone.

Mrs. White stood up and stepped over the front of the wagon, and laying her hand on the haunches of the colt, stepped down onto the shafts.

A Wild Colt Tamed

"Oh, no, you had better not take him," said another. "He isn't safe. He'll hurt someone."

"I think I can manage him," answered James White. "I've broken in several colts to drive, and I think we'll get along all right."

Someone offered Mr. White the use of a market wagon, which had a front and a back seat. It was without a dashboard, and to enter, one had to step up onto an iron step on the shafts and then onto a step that went across the front of the wagon. The colt was brought and hitched to the wagon, and Mr. White got in, holding the reins tight and straight. While someone held the horse's head, Mrs. White sat down beside her husband, and Captain Bates and another brother climbed into the back seat. When all were ready, the colt was let loose, and the party started off. Mr. White had his hands full, but he managed the colt, and they went on their way without any real difficulty.

As they followed the road through the beautiful hills that were aflame with the colors of the late autumn, Mrs. White spoke of the beauties of the new earth and of the joy that will come to all followers of Christ.

While she was talking, the power of God came upon her and she was given a vision. In a beautiful voice she called, "Glory! Glory! Glory!" as she saw the glories of heaven opened before her. As soon as she began to speak, the colt suddenly stopped perfectly still and stood with his head drooped. At the same time, Mrs. White stood up, and with her eyes looking upward, stepped over the front of the wagon, and laying her hand on the haunches of the colt, stepped down onto the shafts.

"That colt will kick her to death!" called out Mr. Bates.

"The Lord has the colt in charge now; I do not wish to interfere," quietly answered Mr. White.

His Messenger

The colt stood as gently as an old horse, as Mrs. White, with her hand on his back, stepped down onto the ground. Mrs. White went up the bank onto a grassy plot beside the road, and walked back and forth while she described the beauties of the new earth.

While Mrs. White was out of the wagon, Mr. White thought he would test the horse to see what was making him so tame. First, he touched the colt with the whip, and it did not move; then Mr. White struck the horse harder and harder, but it remained quiet, just as though it had not even felt the touch of the whip.

"This is a solemn place," said Mr. Bates. "Surely the power that gives the vision, also has subdued the wild nature of this colt."

Then Mrs. White walked slowly down the bank, and again putting her hand on the colt's haunches, stepped back up onto the shafts and into the wagon. When she took her seat, the vision was ended. The colt at once started, and the travelers continued on their journey and reached their destination in safety.

Mr. and Mrs. White went on from church to church, bringing good courage to the believers. Many times meetings were held in a barn, since there were no houses large enough to hold all the people who came together. At times the meetings lasted several days, and the neighbors opened their homes to the visitors, who brought their own bedding and food.

After one meeting had closed, the workers would hurry on to the next place, for they had no time to lose, with so many waiting to hear their message.

The meeting in Port Gibson, New York, lasted longer than they had expected, and Mr. and Mrs. White, accompanied by Captain Bates and another worker, hurried to catch the boat that was to take them on to New York City for a

Sabbath meeting. They reached the landing at the river too late. The boat for New York City had gone. There was another smaller boat going down the river a short distance, and they went on it, expecting to change and take the next boat for the city when it should overtake them.

As the larger boat came near, they called, but the captain would not stop. There was nothing for the travelers to do but to jump from the small boat to the deck of the larger, as the boats were floating near together down the stream. Mr. White jumped onto the low deck of the large boat and then helped Mrs. White to follow him. Captain Bates had the money for their fare in his hand as he jumped to the deck, but the boats had separated a little, and he could not quite make the wide jump. He fell into the dirty water of the river, but immediately he started swimming after the big boat, with the money for their fare in one hand and his pocketbook in the other. His hat came off, and in rescuing it, he lost the fare money. At last the captain of the river boat ordered it to be slowed up, and the dignified Captain Bates was taken aboard, dripping wet, but with his pocketbook held tightly.

It was then impossible to go and fill the appointment in New York, so Mr. White asked the boat captain to let them off at the next village. This he did, and Mr. and Mrs. White, and Captain Bates, who was still drenched, left the boat. At this town lived a few Adventist families, and the travelers went to the home of one of them.

These good people opened up their home to the visitors, and Captain Bates was soon comfortable in dry clothes, while his wet ones were being made fit to wear again.

This unplanned visit proved a great blessing to this family. The mother had been sick for many years, but the workers talked with her and prayed that God would heal her. She

Captain Bates had the money for their fare in his hand as he jumped, but he could not quite make it, for the boats had parted.

was restored to health. Others in the village came in and also received blessing and encouragement from the ministers.

Mr. White felt that as soon as they could they should go on and try to reach their appointment in New York. But when they realized they could not reach the city before the Sabbath, they decided to spend the day with a family of Adventists who lived not far away.

"Here we are," said Captain Bates, when they stopped at the gate in front of the house.

"Let just one of us go to the door first," said Mr. White, "and see if they can keep us; if they can't, we will drive on and spend the Sabbath at a hotel."

When the woman of the house answered his knock, he said, "I am a Sabbathkeeper."

"I am glad to see you. Come in," she said.

"But there are three more in the carriage with me. I thought if we came in together we might frighten you."

"I am never frightened at Christians," was the woman's gentle reply.

The good sister heartily welcomed the travelers. When she was introduced to Captain Bates, she said, "Can this be Brother Bates who wrote that book on the Sabbath question? And come to see us? I am unworthy to have you come under my roof. But the Lord has sent you to us, for we are all starving for the truth."

The next day was a wonderful Sabbath for this family as they gathered in their neighbors to hear the words of truth. The travelers were sure that God had led them in this way, for here were people hungry to hear their message.

When the men turned to look at Mrs. White, they saw that she was still kneeling by the bed, looking upward, for she was in vision.

When God Speaks

JOHN N. LOUGHBOROUGH, an earnest, energetic young First-day Adventist preacher, was traveling through the New England States holding meetings, but the more he studied the Bible, the more dissatisfied he was with the message he was giving.

At one time he came to a town where a Seventh-day Adventist was preaching, and decided to go and hear this minister. Mr. Loughborough became greatly interested in the studies given concerning the seventh-day Sabbath. After the meeting he went back to his room and studied the texts about the Sabbath and the law of God.

"The seventh day must be the true Sabbath," he decided. "The Lord is with these people, and I want to be with them too. I want to know more about what the Bible teaches."

The Adventists were holding their services in the home of one of their members at that time, and the little company heartily welcomed the earnest young preacher to their meetings. The first Sabbath that John Loughborough met with them, Mr. and Mrs. White were also present.

In another room of the house lay a man who was ill with pleurisy. The doctor had said that the man must die, that he could do nothing more for him. During the service the sick man lay in great agony, hardly able to draw another breath, and at the close of the meeting he sent in a request that prayer be offered for him.

Because John Loughborough was a minister, he was invited to go in with Mr. and Mrs. White to pray for the sick man. They bowed by the bedside and prayed earnestly that God would heal the sick. Those bowed in prayer could feel the presence of God in the room, and as they prayed, the sick man was healed. When they arose from prayer, he was sitting up in bed, striking his sides that had been so painful, and saying, "I am fully healed! I shall be able to work tomorrow!"

When the men turned to look at Mrs. White, they saw that she was still kneeling beside the bed, looking upward. The same blessing that had healed the man had fallen upon her, and she was in vision.

"Ellen is in vision," quietly said her husband. "She does not breathe while in this condition."

Mrs. White still knelt beside the bed while she looked upward at something in the distance. She was looking with a natural, pleasant expression. She turned her head from side to side as if she were looking at different objects. Sometimes she moved her hands in a graceful gesture, pointing in the direction she was looking, or clasping them together. Sometimes she spoke, exclaiming in wonder at some beautiful scene she was viewing.

She remained kneeling beside the bed for more than an hour, and all this time she never drew a breath. No air entered or left her lungs.

When the vision was ended, she told those who were with her of what she had seen. She had a special message for Mr. Loughborough, which told him of the struggles he had been having in his work, and of his desire to find the Bible truth. She even described his thoughts.

When God Speaks

"Indeed, there is a power more than human connected with this vision," Mr. Loughborough humbly said.

Daniel said that when he was given a vision, there remained no strength in him. He said, "Straightway there remained no strength in me, neither is there breath left in me." Then a man came and touched him, and he was strengthened.

When the angel of God spoke to Ellen White in vision, she also often became weak, and then was strengthened as the power of God came upon her. One of the most remarkable evidences of divine power was the fact that she, like Daniel, did not breathe. Not a particle of air passed through her lips during the time she was in vision. Even though she told of the things she saw, she spoke without breath. Of course, this would be impossible except for the fact that some power other than her own was in control.

The Lord spoke to Ellen White in several ways. Sometimes she was given a vision while in the presence of other people, at which times she did not breathe and she was given special strength. The visions seemed to be given in this way especially to help people who were doubtful that God could speak in such a way.

More often than any other way, the Lord spoke to her in a dream. During the night the messenger angel would show her many important things. She often said, "In the night season one stood by me and spoke." The believers knew that the one who spoke was the messenger of God. It was in these two ways that the Lord spoke in the days of long ago. He said to the people of Israel, "If there be a prophet among you, I the Lord will make myself known unto him in a vision, and will speak unto him in a dream" (Num. 12:6).

Sometimes the visions given in the presence of others were quite impressive to those who did not know of how God spoke, and such visions helped them to believe that it really

His Messenger

was the power of God that controlled Ellen White and showed her how to work for others.

Once Mr. and Mrs. White were visiting in the home of John Byington, one of the workers. With them at worship was a young woman who was a friend of the family. She was a beautiful, intelligent young woman, who could be a fine worker in the cause of God if she would give her heart to Him. But she had not been willing to keep the Sabbath. The family she was visiting were eager for her to make the right step, but still she held back.

During family worship Mrs. White was given a vision about Sabbathkeeping. She was also shown the young woman and her hesitancy in accepting the Sabbath.

When the vision was ended, Mrs. White reached for the hand of the young woman whom she had never seen until that evening, and calling her by name, she said, "Will you keep the Sabbath?" The young woman hesitated.

"Will you keep the Sabbath?" Mrs. White repeated.

"I will," the girl earnestly responded. And as long as she lived, she never forgot how the Lord had known her by name and had called her through His prophet.

When asked concerning her visions, Ellen White said, "When the Lord sees fit to give a vision, I am taken into the presence of Jesus and angels, and am entirely lost to earthly things. I can see no farther than the angel directs me. My attention is often directed to scenes occurring on earth.

"At times I am carried far ahead into the future and shown what is to take place. Then again I am shown things as they have occurred in the past. After I come out of vision I do not at once remember all that I have seen, and the matter is not so clear before me until I write; then the scene rises before me as was presented in vision, and I can write with freedom.

"Sometimes the things that I have seen are hid from me

When God Speaks

after I come out of vision, and I cannot call them to mind until I am brought before a company where that vision applies; then the things I have seen come to my mind with force. I am just as dependent upon the Spirit of the Lord in relating or writing a vision, as in having the vision. It is impossible for me to call up things that have been shown me unless the Lord brings them before me at the time when He is pleased to have me relate or write them."

James White cheerfully carried his supplies in a bag over his back, right through the town where he had preached.

Carrying the Message

"WILL you not come and live in part of our house?" Stockbridge Howland said to James White. "Some of the other Sabbathkeepers here in Topsham have a little furniture to spare. We would like to have you and Mrs. White come and be with us."

Gladly James and Ellen White accepted this generous offer. They had a new responsibility now, since a little son, Henry, had been born to them. Although they spent nearly all their time traveling, visiting, and teaching the people, still, with their little boy, they needed a place to call home. In the house of the Howlands they were comfortable, though their home was far from elegant.

James White had a courageous, independent spirit. God had called him to the work of the ministry and had sent messages to him telling of the work that he must do in teaching the Bible to others. But even so, James White still felt that he must support his family and not call upon others to help. There were many who had money who would have helped had they known the need in the family, but James and Ellen White carried their responsibility without telling others of their needs.

Constantly calls were sent asking Mr. and Mrs. White to come and preach to some little company of believers that were

His Messenger

hungry to hear the Bible truths. The faithful workers answered all the calls they could, but soon letters began to come asking them to go to other States and hold meetings. They had no money to pay their fare, and Mrs. White felt that it was impossible for her to travel with her small baby. They sent word to the little companies that were calling for meetings that the way was not open for them to come.

That winter, money was very scarce in the humble home of James White. In these early times there was no regular plan for supporting our ministers. One day, when all the food in the house was gone, he walked three miles in the rain to get some money that was due him for labor, and to buy some food. But the man for whom he had worked could give him only a little money, and so Mr. White could not buy much food to take home. He bought a few beans, a little meal and rice, and a few pounds of flour. He put these in a bag and carried them on his back. On his way home he passed through the town of Brunswick, where a few years before he had held meetings, and was known as a preacher. One might think that he would be ashamed and hurt to be seen going through the street with this load. But he was not downhearted. He entered his home courageously singing, "I'm a pilgrim, and I'm a stranger."

His poor wife, however, could not feel so cheerful at first. She was shocked to think that he had been able to draw so little money from his employer and could bring home so little food.

"Has it come to this? Has God forsaken us?" she said.

Mr. White lifted his hand and said, "Hush, the Lord has not forsaken us. He gives us enough for our present wants. Jesus fared no better." Then Mrs. White was sorry that she had shown her discouragement. "Yes," she answered. "And sufferings and trials bring us near to Jesus. The Lord is trying

Carrying the Message

us for our own good. He is stirring up our nest, lest we settle down at ease. Our work is to labor for souls."

In a few days little Henry was taken ill, and rapidly grew worse. The mother and father were much alarmed as they saw their baby lying unconscious, with his breathing quick and heavy. They tried all the remedies that they knew, but he still grew worse. They then called in a nurse, who said that she did not think the baby would get well. They had prayer for him, but still there was no change for the better. The mother then realized that she had made the child an excuse for not traveling and laboring for the good of others as much as they had been called to do. Again they knelt and prayed for the life of their little son, promising God that if He would heal the child, they would go wherever they were needed, trusting in Him always.

They prayed earnestly until they felt that a light from heaven was shining upon them, and from that hour the child began to recover.

"Can you not come and hold a meeting with us in Connecticut?" came a call one day.

Although they had no money on hand to pay the fare, and hardly enough to buy the food they needed, Mr. White replied, "Yes, we will come." He thought they might save the money to pay the fare out of what he would earn. He was then cutting wood for only twenty-five cents a cord. To make it seem still harder, he developed rheumatism, and night after night he was unable to sleep because of the pain. He and his wife both prayed faithfully that God would relieve the pain and give him strength to work; and God did bless him, for he was able to keep on working.

"Wife," said Mr. White, "we must keep five dollars on hand, and even if we get short of food, we must not use that."

Sometimes they felt the lack of food, but still they were de-

The men put the minister in the lead. This was the hardest place, for he had to keep ahead of all the others.

Carrying the Message

termined to save the money for the fare. When Mr. White came to settle with his employer, he had ten dollars left. With this they purchased their tickets and a little necessary clothing to make the journey to Connecticut.

After the meetings were over, they remained in Connecticut for a while, and Mr. White looked about for some way to earn money with which to buy needed food and clothing and other necessary supplies.

He was offered work in the harvest field cutting grain, and although it was harder work than he was accustomed to, he started in at once.

James White had suffered an injury that made it hard for him to do work which required much walking. When he was just a young man, he was cutting heavy timber, when the ax slipped and severed a piece of his ankle bone. The tendons had grown stiff, and he had not been able to bear his weight upon the heel of his right foot for years.

When Mr. White went to the field to work, he found that there were several other men working there who were rough and irreligious. They did not like the idea of having a preacher working with them.

"He's not used to this hard work," one of the men said. "Let's run him down and drive him from the field."

Of course, James White did not know of their feelings, but he himself realized that this heavy work was too hard for him. Before he had gone into the field he had prayed that God would give him the strength to do the work and earn the money.

When he entered the field, the men all waited to start the work together. They each were given a long scythe and were told to cut a swath across the field. They were to work, one following the other, so that each would begin his strip of grain where the other left off. The men put the minister in the

His Messenger

lead. This was the hardest place, for the leader had to keep ahead of all the others and set the pace for the mowers.

Mr. White cut a wide swath, and swung his scythe as fast as he could. The other men who followed him took narrower swaths, and kept as close to him as possible. When Mr. White felt them crowding behind him, he tried to work even faster than he had before. Across the wide field they all worked. At the far end, after a short rest, they turned and started back, with the minister still ahead of the men. When they reached the starting place, the men threw down their scythes.

"White," their leader said, "do you mean to kill yourself and us? We give up this trial. We thought you were a minister, and could not know by experience how to handle a scythe, but we give you the credit of being far ahead of us and the best mower we ever saw."

"And you have taken no beer or liquor this hot day," added another of the rough men.

"When you came into this field as a worker, we were angry," went on the leader. "We didn't want a minister in our company, and we agreed to give you the hardest place. You have gone steadily on, and we have had to give up. We crown you as a leader and a captain in the field."

Mr. White quietly thanked them for the compliment, but he felt that he had One to thank whom they did not love, trust, or serve—the God of heaven.

That day's work proved to be a blessing in more ways than one. It broke down the prejudice of the men of the neighborhood that they had felt toward him because he was a minister, and the severe strain of working so hard in the heat of the day relaxed the tendons of his ankle, and he found himself bringing his heel down squarely on the ground. After this he stepped so firmly no one would ever imagine he had walked with a limp for many years.

Carrying the Message

A few weeks later an urgent invitation came for Mr. and Mrs. White to go to New York and hold a series of meetings among the believers.

"What can we do?" Ellen White asked her husband. "We have no money to pay our fare to New York." Together they prayed that God would open the way.

"I know what I will do," exclaimed James White, after they had finished praying. "I'll buy a scythe and work again in the harvest field. I can earn enough money there to take us to the meeting." This time he worked with Adventist neighbors, and during the next few weeks earned forty dollars, which was used in making the trip to New York to attend the meetings.

At another time a letter came bearing an invitation for them to go to a general meeting that was to be held in a distant town, and again they had no money. When Mr. White went back to the post office he found a letter containing five dollars. He hurried home, and together they knelt and offered a prayer of thanksgiving. Then they started on the journey.

Together Mr. and Mrs. White traveled from place to place, even during the winter. Sometimes they took their little son with them, but much of the time they left him at home. The eldest daughter of the Howlands took upon herself the responsibility of caring for him, and as he grew older, she cared for him almost constantly.

Edson, the second son, was born in 1849. He was only a few weeks old when his mother began taking him with her on her trips to visit the groups of Sabbathkeepers.

Ellen White was especially led to visit the small companies of Sabbathkeepers who were just learning to serve the Lord. She was often directed by a vision to visit where her work was especially needed. Sometimes she would mention a certain little church to her husband, and say, "James, in the night I was bearing testimony to that company. I know the people there need help, and we must visit them." When they would arrive at the meetinghouse, some of the company would come forward and greet them, saying, "You have come at just the right time."

When Edson was a few months old, his mother left him with some friends, who were very kind to the baby. Although the children were well cared for, it was hard for these young parents to leave their little sons. Sometimes they would not see them for weeks at a time.

"Recently, I had the privilege of being with my older boy two weeks," Ellen White wrote to a friend. "He is a lovely dispositioned boy, and he became so attached to his mother it was hard to be separated from him. My other little one is many hundreds of miles from me."

Many people whom they visited did not realize what it meant to this mother to be separated from her children. Once when the Whites had just completed a long journey and were tired out, they stopped at the home of one of the believers. In the morning Mrs. White felt that she could no longer stand to be away from her children. She especially missed her baby, who was only nine months old. With tears she prayed that God would watch over her little sons, and make her willing to sacrifice the pleasure of being with them, for the cause of God.

When she went downstairs, the woman with whom she was staying greeted her. "It must be very pleasant to be riding through the country with nothing to trouble you," the woman said to her guest. "It is just such a life as I would delight in."

"Is this what everyone thinks?" thought the poor, lonesome mother. "No one has the least idea of the self-denial and sacrifice required to travel from place to place, often meeting cold hearts, distant looks, and severe speeches, while my heart is yearning for my home and my little ones."

The next day they started on to another appointment. In

Carrying the Message

the train Mrs. White was so weak and ill that she could not sit up, and her husband made a bed on the seats of the car for her. She lay down with aching head and heart. The lack of sympathy from the believers was hard for her to bear.

"It doesn't pay!" she said to herself that night. "So much labor to accomplish so little." Soon she fell asleep and dreamed that a tall angel stood by her side.

"Why are you sad?" he questioned.

"I can do so little good," she told him. "Why may we not be with our children, and enjoy their company?"

"You have given to the Lord two beautiful flowers," the angel said gently, "the fragrance of which is as sweet incense before Him, and is more precious in His sight than gold or silver, for it is a heart gift. It draws upon every fiber of the heart as no other sacrifice can.

"The path shall brighten before you," he continued. "Every self-denial, every sacrifice, is faithfully recorded and will bring its reward."

The next morning the three horses were brought to the crossroads just as Mrs. White had seen them in vision.

Charlie Takes Them Through

"I AM worried about Mrs. White," said a woman to her neighbor who sat in the back of the meetinghouse. "She is so tired and worn she can scarcely stand."

"Yes," said the neighbor, "she and her husband travel nearly all the time, going from place to place to hold meetings. The stages go slowly and stop so often that it takes hours and hours to go only a few miles; and the train isn't much better. One has to wait a long time at the junctions where a change of cars is made too." She sighed. "They will soon wear out and be able to visit us no more, I fear."

Mr. and Mrs. White were attending meetings in Sutton, Vermont. Mrs. White was extremely tired. She could scarcely stand to speak.

One of the women spoke to her husband about it. "What they need," he answered, "is a good horse and a covered buggy of their own. Then they could travel much faster and safer than by stage. They could stop when they please, and go across country if they wanted to, and save much time."

At once he began talking to other men attending the meetings. "A horse and buggy is what they need," he told them. "They are too poor to buy one of their own. Why can't we take up a collection and buy them one?"

The idea struck them all as being just the right thing to do,

His Messenger

and before long the hat was being passed. When the money was counted, with a few promises added from those who did not have very much money with them, there was $175! What a fine sum of money! Several of the men who had horses for sale agreed each to bring a horse to a certain place on Monday morning and let Mr. and Mrs. White choose the one that they liked best. Of course, the tired workers were surprised and delighted to hear that they were to have a horse of their own to drive. They knew better than anyone else how tiresome it was riding on the train and in the stagecoach.

Sunday night Mrs. White was given a vision in which she saw a group of men gathered at the crossroads. They were holding three horses that they had brought for Mr. White to inspect. The first one brought forward was a high-spirited, nervous sorrel. As they were looking at the horse, the angel who was acting as their guide said to Mrs. White, "Not that one." Then the man showed them a large gray horse that was clumsy and awkward, and again the angel said, "Not that one." The third horse was a beautiful dappled chestnut, a fine, intelligent-looking horse. When he was led forward, the angel said, "This is the one for you."

The next morning Mr. and Mrs. White went to the crossroads where the men were to bring the horses, and the fulfillment of her vision was exact. The same three horses were brought forward for inspection—the nervous sorrel, the clumsy gray, and the dappled chestnut. Of course, it was not hard for Mr. White to make his choice, and soon Old Charlie, the dappled chestnut, was hitched to a good buggy and presented to the delighted workers.

With happy hearts Mr. and Mrs. White went on their way. They were not only happy that they had this comfortable way to travel but they were cheered by the kindness of the good people who had been so thoughtful of their comfort.

Charlie Takes Them Through

It was autumn, and as they traveled over the beautiful hills of New England, the road wound in and out among the trees flaming with autumn colors, and now and then dipped down into a valley where orchards lined the road. Big red apples lay in the path which Old Charlie was following. He soon made known to his new masters that he was fond of apples, and Mr. White unhitched the checkrein so that the horse could lower his head.

Charlie would come trotting down the road until he saw an apple within easy reach, and gently slowing down, he would pick up the apple. Then throwing his head high he would trot on, eating the apple as he went.

At noon they often stopped beside the road to eat their lunch and to rest. Mr. White would spread a blanket on the grass for Mrs. White to rest, and then braid the tall grass and tie the horse to it, so that Charlie might feed and not wander away. During these periods of rest Mr. White was often busy answering letters or writing articles for the paper. He frequently used a box for a writing table, or if he could find nothing better he even laid his paper on the stiff crown of his tall hat.

After a simple lunch and a little rest they thanked God for a safe, pleasant journey, and then traveled on.

Mr. White was so anxious that all his possessions be used in the cause of God that he often lent Old Charlie to other ministers who were called upon to go to some distant place and preach.

One Fourth of July, Mr. Loughborough and another minister started across the country, driving this faithful horse. A heavy rain had been falling, and they found a bridge gone at a stream crossing. Some people living on the bank of the stream told them that teams had been fording the creek; so Mr. Loughborough drove Old Charlie into the water while the

The horse gave two or three more lunges, gained a foothold, and drew the wagon up out of the water.

Charlie Takes Them Through

other minister crossed on a narrow footbridge. In a moment the wagon was floating and the horse was pulled off his feet. Both horse and wagon began to float down the stream. The ministers both lifted their hearts to God, asking that He would save Mr. Loughborough and the faithful horse. As they were being swept down the stream, the wagon wheels struck a large rock. Old Charlie turned his head back and cast a pitiful glance at the driver. "Charlie," called Mr. Loughborough, "you've got to get me out of this!" The horse gave two or three lunges forward with all his might toward the bank. He gained a footing and drew the wagon up out of the water.

A group of people had gathered on the shore when they saw Mr. Loughborough drive the horse into the water, and now they gave a shout of cheer for the brave horse.

The men drove on until they came to a little grove of trees, where they allowed the horse to rest while they gave thanks to God for saving Mr. Loughborough from drowning.

The publishing work was shown to Mrs. White as streams of light that went clear round the world.

The Angel Said, "Write"

WHEN Ellen Harmon had first been told by the angel, "Relate to others that which I have revealed to you," she began to visit groups of believers and tell them her message. Soon after this the angel told her, "Write the things that are revealed to you."

"Lord," she answered, "I cannot write."

She was still suffering from the accident that came to her when she was nine years old, and she could not hold her hand steady.

"Write out the things I give you," the angel again commanded.

With her trembling right hand she took up a pen and began slowly to write. Although her hand had trembled so, that for many months she had not been able to write more than a few words at a time, she obeyed the command of the angel and could now write steadily and clearly.

Ellen White knew that this power to write was a gift from God, and she did not spare herself in using it to His glory. Many letters of guidance were written to the leaders of the different companies to help them in their work.

The visions that were given to her must be shared with the churches too, and these were copied over and over again by hand and sent to different ones of the ministers and faithful workers who could pass them on to others. But this work of writing became a great burden, for there was never enough time to answer all the letters when they should be answered, or to send to each little church the messages that would be a special help to it.

The burden became almost more than Mrs. White and her husband could bear. They prayed for some way to open by which they could reach more people in a shorter length of time without wearing themselves away trying to do more than they could.

A meeting was held in Massachusetts, where a few of the believers gathered to help one another plan the great work of telling others of the seventh-day Sabbath and the nearness of Jesus' coming. During this meeting Ellen White was given a vision of the proclaiming of the message.

After the vision she said to her husband, "I have a message for you. You must begin to print a little paper, and send it out to the people. Let it be small at first; but as the people read, they will send you means with which to print, and it will be a success from the first. From this small beginning it was shown to me to be like streams of light that went clear round the world."

This was indeed an encouraging message! These papers which they were to publish would take the important light to many people. Mrs. White, too, could send out her messages through articles in this paper. How much easier to mail out papers to the different churches than to write a letter to each by hand! Why, even the scattered believers who lived here and there all over the country could have a copy and be blessed by the message.

The plan was wonderful! But no one was willing to put money into this new publishing work. After the meeting James and Ellen White visited different Sabbathkeepers who

The Angel Said, "Write"

had money and farms, but none of them felt that they could spare any money just then for the publishing work.

"I must earn the money myself and publish the paper," Mr. White decided at last. "Last year I earned money by working in the hayfield to pay our fare to visit the churches and attend important meetings. Surely the Lord would bless and strengthen me again for this new work. I will buy a scythe at once and start to work." He and Ellen White were staying with the Beldens in Connecticut at the time, and they agreed to let him mow in their fields. As he started out the door to go to town, someone called, "Mr. White, come back quickly; your wife has fainted."

When James White saw his wife, he realized that her condition was serious. He quickly gathered together those who were in the house, and they earnestly prayed that God would revive Mrs. White. She began to feel better in a few minutes, and then she was given a vision. In the vision she was shown that it was not God's plan for her husband to work in the hayfield this time.

"He has other work for you to do," Mrs. White told him. "You must write, write, write, and walk out by faith. If you do the will of God and publish the paper, others will send the money for the expense of the printing."

When Ellen White told her husband the message, he again started to town, but not to buy a scythe; he was going to make arrangements to have a paper printed.

He went to the printer in Middletown and explained to him all about what he wanted to do.

"If you print this paper for us you will have to wait for the money. Will you do that?" James White asked. The printer was a generous, kindhearted man. He felt that he could trust a man who was getting out a religious paper, and James White looked honest.

His Messenger

"Yes, I will print the paper for you," he said. "How many do you want?"

"I want one thousand copies, and the paper is to have eight pages." The agreement was made, and James White went home to prepare the material for the paper. Now Mr. White must show his faith by trusting in the Lord for the care of his family, if he was to spend his time in writing. Mr. Belden gave him the use of a large unfinished room over his kitchen and dining room. A young woman who had recently inherited some furniture lent it to them, and they were quickly settled in their new home. Mr. White was soon busily writing the articles for the paper.

When a few articles were written, he walked to Middletown, eight miles away, and gave them to the printer. In a few days, when the proof sheets were ready, he went back to the printer again and brought them home, where he and his wife carefully corrected them. The corrected proof sheets were then taken back to Middletown.

What rejoicing there was when the first copy of *Present Truth* was brought home from the printers! Everyone in the house gathered around to see the new paper. The thousand copies were laid upon the floor, and they knelt around them and offered prayer—a prayer of thanksgiving that the truth was at last in print, and a prayer of blessing on the little papers that were to carry God's message from place to place.

The papers were folded and wrapped and addressed to people who they hoped would appreciate their message, and James White carried them to the post office in Middletown. Soon letters began coming back, bringing thanks for the paper and money to pay for the printing. But best of all were the letters telling of people who had learned to keep the seventh-day Sabbath from reading the message found in *Present Truth*.

The Angel Said, "Write"

Three more numbers were printed and sent out in the next three months. Although the paper was small in size and the type was so fine that it was hard to read, still people were eager for the message. More and more letters came asking for papers, which were gladly sent out.

In the late winter James White felt they should change their home to Oswego, New York, for this seemed a better place from which to publish the paper. Then, too, there were several small companies of Adventists living nearby, who needed the help that these workers could give them.

At times the money was slow in coming in to pay for the printing of the paper, and this made it hard for Mr. White. He was working constantly, visiting the people, and writing, and this extra worry made his burdens too heavy.

"I am going to stop the publishing work for a time," wrote Mr. White to a friend. "To publish is an uphill work unless there are many who are interested in the paper and are praying for it." But a few days later, while they were praying for their sick child, Mrs. White was shown in a vision that Mr. White should not be discouraged.

"I saw the paper and that it is needed," she said. "Souls are hungry for the truth that must be written in the paper. God does not want you to stop yet. You must write, write, write, and speed the message. I saw that it will go where God's servants cannot go."

This message encouraged Mr. White, and he changed his plans and went on getting out the paper. In November, 1850, a larger paper was started to take the place of *Present Truth*. This was called *The Second Advent Review and Sabbath Herald,* and was printed in Paris, Maine. Although this paper was much larger than the little *Present Truth,* it also was sent out free. "Terms: gratis, except the reader desires to aid in its publication," was printed in the paper.

His Messenger

The believers everywhere were glad to receive this paper, and many sent in money to help in printing it. But Mr. White worked too hard in getting the articles ready. He could not sleep well, and soon he became very weak. Then, too, in trying to save money, he had not eaten as much food as he should have had to give him the strength he needed. He was hardly able to walk to the printing office. Again he felt discouraged.

"Wife," he said one day, "it is no use to try to struggle on any longer. These things are crushing me, and will soon carry me to the grave. I cannot go on. I have written a note for the paper stating that I shall publish no more."

The next morning while they were bowed in prayer at family worship, Mrs. White was given a vision about this matter.

"I was shown that you must not give up the paper," she told her husband after the vision was ended. "This is just the step that Satan is trying to drive you to take. You must continue to publish, and the Lord will sustain you."

This message gave new courage to Mr. White to continue publishing the *Review and Herald,* but he saw that he could not go on with the work unless he had some help.

Soon after this they moved again, this time to Rochester, New York. Mr. White bought a printing press and type, so that they could do their own printing. He found other workers who were willing to join them in the work of printing the paper, until quite a family lived together. All these workers labored as did Mr. and Mrs. White, without pay except for their food, home, and other necessary expenses, which were met by the donations sent in by the readers of the paper.

The work of these laborers was much appreciated, for although there was no price paid for the papers, still enough money was sent in to support the work. Four men who had fine farms worth about $3,500 each, sold their farms and gave

The Angel Said, "Write"

part of the money for the printing work. The farmers then rented farms or else went into other work.

A paper just for the young people and the boys and girls! That was the desire of Mr. and Mrs. White. Their hopes really came true in August, 1852, when they were able to publish a paper called *The Youth's Instructor* and send it out to the young people.

How they read and treasured every page! In many issues there were articles written by Ellen G. White just for the boys and girls, in language they could understand.

The Youth's Instructor was published every month and mailed to anyone who was interested in having it. Each one who received it was asked to pay twenty-five cents a year.

This paper for young people has been published for more than one hundred years. Now it is sent out to many thousands, and each week it carries its message to every continent.

The car in which they were riding was on the track and back from the wreckage about a hundred feet.

An Angel Uncouples the Train

"I FEEL strange about starting on this trip," James White said to his wife, "but, Ellen, we have an appointment and *we must go.*"

They were staying in the home of Mr. Palmer in Jackson, Michigan, but had planned to take the train that evening for Wisconsin. All afternoon Mr. White moved about restlessly, and several times he spoke of his uneasy feelings. "If I did not have an appointment I would not go tonight," he said.

As night came on, all those in the house united in prayer that Mr. and Mrs. White would be kept safely. When they arose from their knees, James White said, "I am ready to go. The Lord will have a care for us and keep us."

They went to the station, and at eight o'clock they boarded the train and sat down in the first car. James White began to arrange their packages and luggage so that they might be comfortable, but Ellen White looked around with uneasiness. "James," she said, "I can't stay in this car. I must get out of here."

They quickly picked up their bundles and went back into the next car. Mrs. White chose a seat in the middle of the car and sat down with her packages in her lap. "I don't feel at home on this train," she said. They both sat quietly, waiting for something, they did not know what.

His Messenger

The bell rang, and the train started out in the darkness, but it had gone only about three miles when it began to jerk backward and forward and tip sideways. Hastily they raised the window and looked out. They saw the car in front standing on end, and the air was filled with cries and groans. The engine, too, was lying off the track. But the car in which they were riding was on the track and back from the wreckage about a hundred feet. The express car was crushed to pieces, but the baggage car, which held a big trunk of books and papers belonging to Mr. White, was only slightly damaged, and the trunk was safe.

The car in which Mr. White had first found seats was crushed, and the wreckage, together with the injured people, was thrown on each side of the track.

Another train was expected in a few minutes, and everyone was very much excited. Pieces of the wreckage were quickly gathered into a pile and set afire to warn the oncoming train, while some of the men took burning pieces of wood for torches and hurried down the track to meet the train.

James White took his wife in his arms, and wading in the water, carried her across a small stream and a swampy field to the main road. They walked on a half mile down the road until they came to a house. Here Mrs. White waited while her husband went on with a messenger from the train wreck, who was being sent to Jackson for a physician. Mr. White found a team of horses and came for his wife, and they both went to the home of one of the Adventists who lived nearby.

The next morning they all went back to see the wreck. They found that a large ox had lain down on the track, and when the engine struck it, the train left the track. The car in which Mr. and Mrs. White had been riding was standing back by itself. It had been uncoupled from the rest of the train, and the coupling bolt with its chain was lying on the

An Angel Uncouples the Train

platform of the car, as though it had been placed there. But the brakeman had not been there, and it was a mystery to the trainmen how it could have happened.

As Mr. and Mrs. White looked at the crushed cars and the overturned engine and then at the last two cars standing safe and undamaged, they said, "God does hear prayer. His angel must have uncoupled that car and preserved the lives of His servants."

In a few hours Mr. and Mrs. White were able to take another train and with their trunk of books continue on their journey. They reached Wisconsin in time for their appointment, happy that they were traveling in the cause of God and that His angel was ever guiding and watching over them. This visit was a great help to the people who were interested in the Advent message in Wisconsin.

Two years before this, Mr. Bates had preached in Battle Creek, and had baptized one man. This man had brought others to unite with him, and there were now several believers. Mr. and Mrs. White visited this little company in Battle Creek. The work grew, and still others joined the Sabbathkeepers there. They urged Mr. and Mrs. White to move to this town and make it their home. After a meeting held by the leading workers it was decided to move the printing house and the press that had recently been bought to Battle Creek. Land was cheap, and the workers in the printing house could have homes of their own here and not live crowded together as they had been living.

In Battle Creek the White family for the first time had a house to themselves. Here they could live with their three sons and have time to rest and study. Any stranger was always made welcome in this home.

Often there were meetings held in Battle Creek, and people came from many miles away and spent the day. Sometimes they brought their bedding and stayed two or three days. The church members in Battle Creek opened up their homes and entertained these visitors. The White home was always open, and visitors were always given a hearty welcome. One day when a general meeting was held in Battle Creek, there were thirty-five guests for dinner. At other times people came and stayed for a week at a time.

A Child Is Lost

THE next spring after the printing press was moved to Battle Creek, a general meeting was appointed for that place. It had been announced in the *Review and Herald* that all were invited to this conference and that the church members of Battle Creek would entertain, as well as they could, all who came.

Every Sabbathkeeper in the town was busy setting his house in order and putting up extra beds, even making places to sleep in the big haymows and in the carriage houses. In the White home every preparation possible was made to accommodate guests.

Willie, the youngest son of Ellen and James White, was less than two years old, and he played about the house, getting in the way as all babies do when extra work is being done. Someone was getting ready to mop the floor, and a large tub of water had been placed in the middle of the kitchen floor. The girl who helped with the housework and cared for the baby hurried through the kitchen, but a gurgling sound attracted her attention and she turned to look back. A little foot was sticking out of the tub of water. She ran across the room, pulled the baby from the water, and rushed with him to his mother. "He's drowned! He's drowned!" she screamed.

Ellen White took her baby and ran into the yard with him

and laid him on the grass. "Call James White and send for the doctor," she said. The girl ran to the front of the house, where she saw one of the pressmen who happened to be passing by. She called to him, "Run for the doctor." But this she felt was not enough to do; so she ran after him, hitting the surprised man on the back at every step and shouting, "Run, run, run." Of course, the man ran with great speed, and the girl came back to see what more she could do to make up for her neglect in not watching the baby.

Ellen White cut off his wet clothes and laid Willie on the grass and rolled him back and forth. Neighbors who gathered told her it was of no use, that the baby was dead, but with a constant prayer on her lips she kept on working over the child. Finally she took him in her arms, and as she kissed him, his eyelids flickered and he puckered his little lips to return her kiss. With a glad heart she took him into the house and laid him in his little crib and put warm cloths around him. And before the doctor came, he was breathing naturally again.

That night Ellen White lay in her bed with her little one in her arms. She rejoiced that God had spared his life and returned him to them again. With a thankful heart she praised her Saviour. Suddenly on the clear night air sounded the sharp ringing of the bells and a cry, "Lost! Lost! A child lost!"

She held her little one closer as she thought of how that day he had almost been lost, and of the vacant place there would have been in his little cradle and in their own hearts if he had not been restored to them. The meaning of the word *lost* came home to her with a force it had never had before.

"Never shall I forget the incidents of that night," she wrote later. "It was just one little life that was at stake; but it seemed as though the whole city of Battle Creek was stirred

A Child Is Lost

to go out in search of the lost child. Lights were glimmering everywhere. They flashed through the streets, along the riverbank, and through the adjacent woods, and the cry resounded, 'A child is lost! A child is lost!' After a long search, a shout was raised, 'The child is found!'

"Yes, the child was found; but it might go astray on the journey of life and be lost at last.

"I knew, too, that death might come to the little one that was saved to me; and that should he live, he would have the evils of this life to battle with. And the thought with me was, Will this little child, whose life I hold so dear, be finally lost, or will he be saved to praise God forever in His kingdom?

"There was no sleep for my eyes that night. I thought of the lost sheep that Jesus came from heaven to earth to seek and to save. I thought of Christ as He looked down from heaven upon a world of lost sinners, lost without hope, and of the sympathy that led Him to leave His high and exalted place upon His Father's throne, and make the infinite sacrifice necessary to lift man up from the degradation of sin, and bring him back to the fold of God."

Across the Mississippi

AT THE time the work was being started in Battle Creek, some of the Sabbathkeepers from Maine and other parts of New England decided to move out across the Mississippi to the new country of Iowa.

"You can buy good, fertile land cheap here," wrote one of the friends who had just moved out West. "The country is prairie, and there are no stumps or stones to clear away."

"This sounds good to me," said one of the hard-working men who had lived on a rocky farm in Maine all his life.

"And too, we can spread the gospel message out there," a young minister said. "We can support ourselves with ease, and have much time left for gospel work." Several families decided to go to Waukon, Iowa, and take their oxen and farm tools with them.

They were soon settled on the new land and were busy building homes. But the work was not as easy as they had thought it would be. They toiled from early until late, but it was not long before they realized that the glowing promises of the friends who had first moved to the West were not all going to prove true. The minister turned to carpenter work to support his family, and preaching was forgotten. All these hardships brought discouragement. The families who had been old friends in Maine, began to criticize one another and to find fault. The little church that had been formed was almost broken up by discouragement and faultfinding.

In the middle of the winter Mr. and Mrs. White were holding some meetings in Illinois. While there, Mrs. White was given a vision concerning this little company of believers in Waukon, Iowa. She felt that she must visit them as soon as possible and bring them spiritual help and encouragement.

"We must go and visit the believers in Waukon," she told her husband. "They need our help."

"It is two hundred miles from here," said Mr. White, "and the trip will have to be made in an open sleigh; but if you feel that we are needed there, we will go."

They asked two of the men who were working with them in Illinois to find a sleigh and take them to Iowa. These men felt that they could not refuse to share the hardship with Mrs. White if she was determined to go, but they knew it was a long, dangerous journey to be taken in the middle of winter when the ground was covered deep with snow.

The afternoon before the four people planned to start on the trip, rain began to fall. By night the snow was fast melting away, and they realized that it would be impossible to use a sleigh in the mud and water.

One of the men turned to Mrs. White and said, "Mrs. White, what about Waukon?"

She answered, "We shall go."

"Yes," he replied, "if the Lord works a miracle."

Many times during the night Mrs. White rose and went to the window to watch the weather. About daybreak a cold wind began to blow, and snow fell thick and white. By five o'clock the next afternoon the roads were good enough for them to start with the sleigh.

As they traveled northward, the snow continued to fall until the roads were almost blocked. The second night they

stopped at the home of Sabbathkeepers in Green Vale. The next morning they found the roads in every direction covered with heavy drifts of snow. For nearly a week they waited here for the roads to be opened. When they felt that it was possible to travel they started on again, but progress was slow. Many times they had to dig a way through the snowdrifts.

Thursday evening they stayed at a hotel a few miles from the great Mississippi River. There was no bridge across the river, but teams crossed on the firm ice. Although this ice was covered with snow, it was thought to be quite strong.

About four o'clock the next morning Mrs. White was awakened by the sound of rain falling on the roof. At once they arose and gathered their things together, ready to travel on. They dared not wait, for the rain would weaken the ice on the river. In the light of the early dawn they rode in the open sleigh toward the river, with the cold rain drenching

"We have come to the Red Sea," he shouted. "Shall we go across?"

them. There had been a crust of ice over the snow that made it easy for the horses to walk and for the sleigh to slip over the snow, but the rain melted the ice until the horses' hoofs broke through the crust at every step.

When James White and his companions reached the river, they asked if it was possible to cross, but no one whom they asked would give them any encouragement. The ice on the river was soft and spongy and mixed with snow, and a foot of water stood on top of it. They stopped at the edge of the water. One of the men stood up in the sleigh.

"We have come to the Red Sea," he shouted. "Shall we cross?"

"Go forward, trusting in Israel's God," his companions answered.

Slowly they drove the team onto the ice. They crossed the river, praying as they went, and were carried safely over the treacherous ice. As the team pulled the sleigh up the bank on the Iowa side of the river, they all united in praising God.

A group of people stood watching them cross. "No amount of money would tempt me to venture out on that ice," said one of them. But God's followers were safe in going where He sent them. No ordinary business would have made them take such a risk.

The travelers went to a hotel not far from the river and prepared to spend the Sabbath. In the evening they sat in the parlor of the hotel and sang hymns, while the other guests gathered to listen. The listeners expressed their appreciation of the songs; then one of the ministers hung up his prophetic chart and gave a short lecture. When it was time to separate for the night, the travelers were invited to stop on their way back from Waukon and give another lecture.

Early Sunday morning the sleigh was prepared, and the journey was begun again. It was a bitter-cold day, and the travelers were continually in danger of freezing. They all watched one another to see if a nose or an ear was freezing.

"Brother, your face is freezing, you had better rub the frost out as soon as possible," one would say to another.

This weather lasted for three more days, and they suffered much. Thursday morning Ellen White wrote to her children:

"Here we are fourteen miles this side of Waukon. We are all quite well. Have had rather a tedious time getting thus far. Yesterday for miles there was no track. Our horses had to plow through snow, very deep, but on we came.

"Oh, such fare as we have had on this journey! Last Monday we could get no decent food, and tasted not a morsel, with the exception of a small apple, from morn until night. We have most of the time kept very comfortable, but it is the bitterest cold weather we ever experienced.

Across the Mississippi

"We introduce our faith at every hotel we enter, and have some two or three invitations to hold meetings on our return.... There seems to be interest awakened at every place we stop. We think we shall have some meetings in this place next first day....

"O how thankful shall I be to see home, sweet home, again, and my dear little boys, Henry, Edson, and Willie.... Children, be thankful for your comfortable home. We often suffer with cold, and cannot keep warm sitting before the stove....

"Last night we slept in an unfinished chamber where there was an opening for the stovepipe, running through the top of the house—a large space, big enough for a couple of cats to jump out of.

"Pray for us, ... for God to open the way for our return, or we may be blocked in and remain all winter. Pray for the Lord to give us success."

In the afternoon of the day before Christmas the weary travelers reached Waukon. The Sabbathkeepers there were greatly surprised. They had read in the *Review* of the meetings to be held in Illinois, but they had not thought it possible for anyone to travel through the deep snow and the cold to Waukon.

Meetings were appointed at once in the home of Edward Andrews. All the Sabbathkeepers met together to hear the workers who had come to visit them. Discouragement and misunderstanding were wiped away, and wonderful meetings were held. The people who lived in Waukon were blessed as the Spirit of God came upon Mrs. White and she was given a vision. During the vision she solemnly repeated, "Return unto me, and I will return unto you, saith the Lord." This brought a wonderful new hope to those who had been discouraged.

The workers did not stay long, but soon started back over

the same long, cold journey. The Sabbathkeepers in Waukon shed tears when they saw these faithful workers leave.

Although Mrs. White was tired and almost sick from her long journey in the cold without good food, still she wrote, "We are already many times paid for facing the prairie winds and storms on our long and tedious journey to northern Iowa."

Letters to the Boys

"THE neat, orderly, and careful boy has an invariable rule, 'A place for everything and everything in its place.' Go into his room at any hour, you will find everything in order," wrote Ellen White to her boys. Although she was away from them a great deal, she tried to train them in the right way.

"I have just been reading a book entitled, 'How to Be a Man,'" she wrote. "I will copy a few lines, and you can apply as your case is met.

"'He can go in the dark and lay his hands upon anything that he wants,'" her letter continues. "'He never leaves a thing at random where he happens to be using it, but always puts it where it belongs. When he undresses, every article of his clothing is folded and laid together in the order that it will be wanted in the morning, so that he loses no time in hunting for it. He is equally careful of his person. He never considers himself dressed till he has washed his hands and face, cleaned his teeth, and combed his hair; and he never thinks of sitting down to the table with dirty hands.

"'He learns to keep his clothes neat and clean. He never forgets to use the scraper at the door to remove the mud from his feet, and he makes it an invariable rule never to pass a mat without wiping his shoes. He never says, like the sloven, "I didn't think," to excuse himself. He would consider it un-

In her letters to her sons, Mrs. White contrasted a tidy boy with a slovenly boy, and urged them to neatness and order in their personal habits.

pardonable in him *not to think;* for what is the ability of thinking worth, if it never comes when it is wanted?

" 'And home is a delightful place to him, because he meets with smiles and pleasant words. But the sloven exposes himself to sour looks and chiding, by his dirty habits; and he finds home a disagreeable place, because he makes it so.'

"We want you, dear boys, to be patterns of neatness and order. Willie looks to you for example. He has great confidence that you do everything about right.

"We are absent from you much, and you should feel that a responsibility rests upon you, my dear boys, to strictly guard yourselves from falling into wrong habits and also to save Willie from doing wrong.

"A noble example for him will do much to influence him to preserve correct habits. We commit you to God, earnestly praying that His angels guard you all three, and incline your hearts to love Him. Your affectionate Mother."

From the same book, *How to Be a Man,* Ellen White had written to her boys a quotation about a person who is careless in his habits. " 'He leaves a thing where he uses it,' " she copied. " 'Hence if he wants anything, he never knows where to look for it, unless he happens to remember when he used it last. He must waste his time in hunting for it. Hence you will often hear him impatiently inquiring if anyone has seen his things, when he ought himself to know where they are.' "

"Dear children, I do not write merely for your amusement, but for your improvement," the letter continues. "Learn where you fail, and then commence the work of reform in earnest. You must learn order. Have set hours to work in the garden, set hours to read and improve your minds. Spend no precious moments in bickerings and finding fault with each other. This disturbs your own happiness and pleases the enemy.

"Remember the eye of God is ever upon you. Endeavor to please Him in all your acts. Make your peace with Him while you are in health. Your parents have a deep interest in you. Our greatest desire is that you may be subjects of grace. You will never be saved against your will. You must prize salvation, and submit to be saved in the Lord's appointed way. Humble repentance of sin, and faith in Jesus as your Saviour, will be required on your part, and He is faithful that hath promised. He will accept you, and give you of His salvation.

"If you deny yourselves in many things, and refrain from sin for a season only, this will not be sufficient. It is a life of obedience that will please God and be acceptable to Him. Delay not to make an entire consecration to God, that your names may be recorded in the Lamb's book of life. Your affectionate Mother."

The two older boys, who at this time were twelve and fourteen years old, missed their parents a great deal. But they too must sacrifice the company of their parents, and sometimes their home, for the cause of God. They learned to be kind, patient, and helpful wherever they stayed. They must also help in the training of their little brother. Their mother and father especially put this trust upon them, to guide and help the younger brother, who was only about seven years old then.

One time she wrote to Henry, "I hope, dear Henry, that you are a good boy, and are happy doing right. Continue to strive to be faithful in all things. We received your letter, and were much pleased to hear from you. We think you have made improvements in setting type. Be faithful, children, in all things. The Lord will soon come and take the good and holy to Himself.

"We want you to live among the pure and holy angels in heaven, and wear a crown of gold, and eat of the tree of life. Trust in the Lord at all times. Listen to the voice of conscience. Love God, and you will have His approving smile. What a thought, to have the great God, the Maker of heavens and the earth, to smile upon and love you. Dear children, seek for this, pray for it, live for it."

To Willie, her youngest son, she wrote from Iowa:

"My dear Willie: We have not forgotten you, my dear boy. When we see other little children around, we long to get our little Willie in our arms again, and press his little soft cheek and receive his kiss. In about five weeks we shall be at home again, and then, Willie, we will work in the garden, and tend the flowers and plant the seeds. You must be a good, sweet little boy, and love to obey Jenny and Lucinda. *Give up your will,* and when you wish to do anything very much, inquire, 'Is it selfish?'

"You must learn to yield your will and your way. It will be a hard lesson for my little boy to learn, but it will in the end be worth more to him than gold. Learn, my dear Willie, to be patient, to wait others' time and convenience; then you will not get impatient and irritable. The Lord loves those little children who try to do right, and He has promised that they shall be in His kingdom. . . .

"Although He is in heaven, and you cannot see Him, yet He loves you when you do right and writes it down in His book; and when you do wrong, He puts a black mark against your name.

"Now, dear Willie, try to do right always, and then no black mark will be set down against you; and when Jesus comes, He will call for that good boy, Willie White, and will put upon your head a wreath of gold, and put in your hand a little harp that you can play upon, and it will send forth beautiful music, and you will never be sick, never be tempted to do wrong; but will be happy always, and will eat of rich fruit, and will pluck beautiful flowers. Try, try, dear boy, to be good.

"YOUR AFFECTIONATE MOTHER."

Mrs. White tried to train her children to be good, honest, industrious boys. She also taught them to be kind and thoughtful in all their association with one another.

When the boys were leaving home in the morning, she would often say to them: "Now, children, you are going out for a day's work. Remember that you are to guard your tongues. Speak not one word that will provoke a wrong act. If you fail, then when we meet at family worship during the evening hour, we shall talk the matter over and make it right with God. You see, children, kind words never cause you any pain and sorrow. Speak kindly, tenderly, to one another, and see what a refreshing, what a blessing, comes to your own heart. . . . Be brave, be true."

Sometimes during the day one of the children would come to Mrs. White and say, "Mother, someone has done wrong." Or, "Mother, someone hasn't treated me right." Mrs. White would gently reply, "When we come together in the evening, we will talk it over."

When evening came, the children would gather together before going to bed and talk over the happenings of the day with their father and mother. There had been time for them to think over any hasty acts, and they were willing to take more of the blame upon themselves.

"Mother, I have done wrong," one would say. "I feel that I would like to have you ask the Lord to forgive me. I believe He will." Then the family would bow in prayer, confessing the sins of the day and praying for forgiveness. Sometimes there were tears in their eyes as they made each wrong right.

After the record of the day was clear, the boys would lie down to sleep, sure that God had blessed them.

The Narrow Way

A VERY impressive dream was given to Mrs. White while she was living in Battle Creek, Michigan, in 1868. Because this dream would be an encouragement to those who trusted in God, she told the believers about it.

"I dreamed of being with a large body of people," she said. "A portion of this assembly started out prepared to journey. We had heavily loaded wagons. As we journeyed, the road seemed to ascend. On one side of this road was a deep precipice; on the other was a high, smooth, white wall. . . .

"As we journeyed on, the road grew narrower and steeper. In some places it seemed so very narrow that we concluded that we could no longer travel with the loaded wagons. We then loosed them from the horses, took a portion of the luggage from the wagons and placed it upon the horses, and journeyed on horseback.

"As we progressed, the path still continued to grow narrow. We were obliged to press close to the wall, to save ourselves from falling off the narrow road down the steep precipice. As we did this, the luggage on the horses pressed against the wall, and caused us to sway toward the precipice. We feared that we should fall, and be dashed in pieces on the rocks. We then cut the luggage from the horses, and it fell over the precipice. We continued on horseback, greatly fear-

His Messenger

ing, as we came to the narrower places in the road, that we should lose our balance, and fall. At such times, a hand seemed to take the bridle, and guide us over the perilous way.

"As the path grew more narrow, we decided that we could no longer go with safety on horseback, and we left the horses and went on foot, in single file, one following in the footsteps of another. At this point small cords were let down from the top of the pure white wall; these we eagerly grasped, to aid us in keeping our balance upon the path. As we traveled, the cord moved along with us. The path finally became so narrow that we concluded that we could travel more safely without our shoes; so we slipped them from our feet, and went on some distance without them. Soon it was decided that we could travel more safely without our stockings; these were removed, and we journeyed on with bare feet.

"We then thought of those who had not accustomed themselves to privations and hardships. Where were such now? They were not in the company. At every change, some were left behind, and those only remained who had accustomed themselves to endure hardships. The privations of the way only made these more eager to press on to the end.

"Our danger of falling from the pathway increased. We pressed close to the white wall, yet could not place our feet fully upon the path, for it was too narrow. We then suspended nearly our whole weight upon the cords, exclaiming: 'We have hold from above! We have hold from above!' The same words were uttered by all the company in the narrow pathway.

"As we heard the sounds of mirth and revelry that seemed to come from the abyss below, we shuddered. We heard the profane oath, the vulgar jest, and low, vile songs. We heard the war song and the dance song. We heard instrumental music, and loud laughter, mingled with cursing and cries of

The Narrow Way

anguish and bitter wailing, and were more anxious than ever to keep upon the narrow, difficult pathway. Much of the time we were compelled to suspend our whole weight upon the cords, which increased in size as we progressed.

"I noticed that the beautiful white wall was stained with blood. It caused a feeling of regret to see the wall thus stained. This feeling, however, lasted but for a moment, as I soon thought that it was all as it should be. Those who are following after will know that others have passed the narrow, difficult way before them, and will conclude that if others were able to pursue their onward course, they can do the same. And as the blood shall be pressed from their aching feet, they will not faint with discouragement; but, seeing the blood upon the wall, they will know that others have endured the same pain.

"At length we came to a large chasm, at which our path ended. There was nothing now to guide the feet, nothing upon which to rest them. Our whole reliance must be upon the cords, which had increased in size, until they were as large as our bodies. Here we were for a time thrown into perplexity and distress. We inquired in fearful whispers, 'To what is the cord attached?' My husband was just before me. Large drops of sweat were falling from his brow, the veins in his neck and temples were increased to double their usual size, and suppressed, agonizing groans came from his lips. The sweat was dropping from my face, and I felt such anguish as I had never felt before. A fearful struggle was before us. Should we fail here, all the difficulties of our journey had been experienced for nought.

"Before us, on the other side of the chasm, was a beautiful field of green grass about six inches high. I could not see the sun, but bright, soft beams of light, resembling fine gold and silver, were resting upon this field. Nothing I had seen upon

"At length we came to a large chasm, at which our path ended. . . . Our whole reliance must be upon the cords."

earth could compare in beauty and glory with this field. But could we succeed in reaching it? was the anxious inquiry. Should the cord break, we must perish. Again, in whispered anguish, the words were breathed, 'What holds the cord?'

"For a moment we hesitated to venture. Then we exclaimed: 'Our only hope is to trust wholly to the cord. It has been our dependence all the difficult way. It will not fail us now.' Still we were hesitating and distressed. The words were then spoken: 'God holds the cord. We need not fear.' These words were then repeated to those behind us, accompanied with: 'He will not fail us now. He has brought us thus far in safety.'

"My husband then swung himself over the fearful abyss into the beautiful field beyond. I immediately followed. And oh, what a sense of relief and gratitude to God we felt! I heard voices raised in triumph and praise to God. I was happy, perfectly happy.

"I awoke, and found that from the anxiety I had experienced in passing over the difficult route, every nerve in my body seemed to be in a tremor. This dream needs no comment. It made such an impression upon my mind that probably every item in it will be vivid before me while my memory shall continue."

A Christmas Long to Be Remembered

"A SPECIAL burden rests upon me for the young people," Ellen White said to her husband. "I long to see them choose Christ for their Saviour. Let us especially work for them during these meetings that we shall hold."

Appointments had been made for meetings to be held with several churches and companies of Sabbathkeepers. Mrs. White was sick with a severe cold, and as it was winter, some thought she should not go.

"I dare not consult my own feelings," she told these friends. "Our appointments are out, and if it is possible, we must go."

The first day they traveled fifty miles with their horse and buggy to Monterey, Michigan, and they were blessed and strengthened as they went on their journey. The next day they began to hold meetings which were especially for the children and young people. Mrs. White spoke to them on the subject "What Shall I Do to Be Saved?" and all those who wanted to be Christians and desired the prayers of God's people were invited to occupy the front seats.

This was hard for the boys and girls to do. Mrs. White knew that it would be hard for them to rise while everyone was looking at them, and walk down to those front seats.

"If they can only take this first step they will gain strength to take the next," Mrs. White said to her husband as they planned the meeting. "For by so doing they testify to all present that they choose to leave sin and the service of Satan and become Christ's followers."

One after another came forward until nearly the whole Sabbath school who were old enough to know what sin was had filled the front seats. James and Ellen White were so happy that they felt like taking those dear children in their arms and carrying them to the feet of Jesus.

"We feel sure that Jesus would say, 'Son, daughter, thy sins be forgiven thee,'" she said to the children.

When the meeting was over, the boys and girls did not forget that they had promised to follow Jesus. They wanted to be sure that their sins were confessed and forgiven. All those who could, went to the home of one of the believers and held a meeting of their own, where they prayed for one another and for themselves. Later Mr. White spoke to these children on the subject of baptism. Each child rose and with tears gave his testimony that he wished to be a Christian and be baptized. Mrs. White listened with gladness to these testimonies. She felt that the long hard trip they had taken to meet with these people was well worth while. "I believe angels of God bore those short, broken testimonies to heaven, and they were recorded in the books of God's remembrance," she wrote in her diary.

In a few days arrangements were made for a baptism, and ten girls stood ready to enter the water to receive baptism. One of these girls had been so afraid of the water all her life that she could not make herself even come near it. Now she stood with her face turned away from the stream, too frightened to look at the water or watch her friends receive baptism.

All had been baptized except the poor frightened girl, and she turned away, giving up to her terror of the water. Mrs.

One girl was so afraid of the water that she stood with her face turned away from the stream, too frightened to watch her friends receive baptism.

A Christmas Long to Be Remembered

White felt that this was the way Satan had of keeping her from giving herself to Christ, and that if the girl left without being baptized she would never have strength to follow the example of her Saviour. She gently urged the girl to come to the edge of the water. Still she hesitated.

Mr. and Mrs. White walked beside the girl and led her toward the stream while their hearts were lifted up to God to take away her fear of water. Finally the girl stepped to the edge of the stream and dipped her hands into the water. "In the name of the Lord, move forward," said Mr. White. The girl calmly went into the water and was baptized. Calmly she came out of the water, happy that she had overcome her dread.

The next morning the girl came running over to the house where Mr. and Mrs. White were staying. Her face was lighted up with happiness. "I am so glad that you didn't leave me alone, just because I was afraid," she said. "I am happy that I have done this for Jesus." Mr. and Mrs. White were happy, too, that she had won a precious victory over her fears, and had obeyed the Lord's command.

The meetings for young people continued, and the next day five young men were baptized. "It was an interesting sight," Ellen White wrote, "to see these young men as they stood side by side all about of the same age and size, and professing their faith in Christ and taking the solemn vow upon them to leave sin and the world, from henceforth to tread the narrow path to heaven."

Mr. and Mrs. White went on from this place to others, and at each little church where they held meetings especially for the young people many were converted and baptized. When they returned home again they felt that this was indeed a journey never to be forgotten.

Some time after this, Mr. and Mrs. White went to New Hampshire and visited the little church at Washington. At

His Messenger

this place there were a number of children and young people, but none of them were really converted. One strong young man had not given his heart to Jesus because he had seen many faults in the older church members. He knew that his own father, who was the choir leader, had a sin which he thought no one knew anything about. As the young man worked with him in the woods he saw the telltale brown stain in the snow, which his father had tried to cover up; so he knew that he was secretly using tobacco.

At the Sabbath morning meeting Mrs. White spoke to a number of persons that she previously had seen in vision and for whom she had messages of reproof or counsel. While she was speaking, a thought suddenly flashed into the young man's mind. "I wish she would speak to my father and tell him about his sin. I would be sure that no one had told her."

As if in answer to this unspoken wish Mrs. White turned to the father. "Brother," she said, "I was shown your case. You are a slave to tobacco." Then she told of his use of tobacco and of how he was hiding this sin and thought no one knew. She described his feelings and actions even better than he himself could have described them.

The face of the young man lighted up. "Only an angel could have told her that," he thought. "Indeed this message *is* from God."

Among the older members of the church there was a turning to God. They confessed their sins to God and to one another. "Now," said Mrs. White, "we must work especially for the young people. They need our help."

As the meetings were held, one after another the young people gave their hearts to God. At a meeting on Christmas Day thirteen of the children and young men and women rose and expressed the desire to be followers of Christ.

One of the young men who had had no interest in religion

A Christmas Long to Be Remembered

was Fred Mead. He had been what the neighbors called a wild boy. Now he took his stand for Christ in the meeting, and he was eager that others should do as he had done. When his cousin, Orville Farnsworth, the son of William Farnsworth, came to his home to bring Christmas presents for the family, Fred invited him into his room. There he made an earnest appeal to Orville to serve Christ. The boys knelt together by Fred's bed, and while Fred prayed, Orville Farnsworth gave his heart to God.

It was a Christmas long to be remembered, not only by those boys but by the whole church. Before the meetings closed eighteen young men and women and children asked to be baptized and to become members of the church.

Although it was a cold winter, twelve of these young people felt that they wanted to be baptized at once. A river was near, but it was covered with two feet of ice. Not to be discouraged, the young men cut the ice, exposing a little pool of open water. They cut steps in the ice so they could walk down into the water. Then, although the temperature was 10° below zero, those twelve young people were baptized. As soon as they left the water they were wrapped in robes and hurried to a warm home nearby. No one suffered any ill effects from this exposure. In the spring the remaining six were baptized.

What new life this group of earnest young people put into the church as they followed on in their Christian experience, doing what they could in the cause of God!

As these young people became older they took an active part in carrying the message of truth to the world. Three of the young men became presidents of conferences; Fred Mead was a missionary in Africa and died there; two other young men became church elders, and three of the young women were Bible instructors, both in America and in foreign lands. Others have filled more humble places in the work of God.

His Messenger

For several years it was my privilege to have one of these faithful workers, Orville O. Farnsworth, as a neighbor. All have now been laid away to rest and wait until Jesus comes, but their children are carrying the gospel message, and now the grandchildren are serving God as ministers, teachers, Bible workers, and missionaries.

A Stranger Comes to Town

THE westbound train drew up to the station at Battle Creek, Michigan, one June day in 1869. One of the first passengers to get off the train was a slender young man. He stood on the platform and looked about him, but said nothing. Finally, when the passengers had almost all hurried away, he stepped up to the stationmaster and showed him an envelope on which was written, "J. N. Andrews, Battle Creek, Michigan."

"Where are you going?" asked the stationmaster. The stranger smiled and pointed to the envelope. When the stationmaster understood that the young man could not speak English, he asked a friend to take the stranger to the Review and Herald office.

Mr. White met the young man and greeted him in a cordial way that could be understood in any language. He took him to his home, and then sent for a French brother to interpret for the stranger.

"He has come all the way from Switzerland with only this envelope to guide him," the interpreter said. "And he brings greetings from a group of fifty Sabbathkeepers in Switzerland. He has come to learn more of the Sabbath message."

The Adventists in Battle Creek were happy to know that the message of God was spreading to such distant parts. They made the stranger, Jacques Erzenberger, welcome among

The young stranger stood on the station platform and looked about him.

A Stranger Comes to Town

them. He stayed in the home of Mr. and Mrs. White, who were glad to teach him the word of God.

First of all, though, Jacques Erzenberger must be taught English so that he might talk with the family. John Kellogg, then a worker in the Review office, was invited to come to the White home and live with them while he taught English to the overseas guest. The whole family also helped the stranger in the interesting task of learning a new language.

Even the cook took her turn in teaching English; and Willie, who was now fifteen years old, did what he could to help. Every day he spent all the time he could taking Jacques Erzenberger about and naming different objects for him.

This method was successful, for at the end of five weeks Mr. Erzenberger attended a meeting of Adventists held in a grove, and gave an interesting talk in English, which all could understand. In another month he spoke at a camp meeting in Ohio, and gave such an earnest appeal for help for the people of his country that many wept. An offering of seventy-five dollars was taken up at that meeting, the first offering given by Seventh-day Adventists for foreign missions.

Jacques Erzenberger remained in America a year and a half, and then returned to his own country to carry to his people the wonderful truths he had learned here. He earnestly pleaded before he left that a missionary be sent to his country to teach the people. There was no money that could be used to send a teacher with him, so he left with the promise that someday a teacher would come.

A missionary to a foreign land! Yes, at last the Seventh-day Adventists were to have a foreign missionary. In 1874, nearly four years after Jacques Erzenberger went back to Europe, J. N. Andrews sailed across the Atlantic to start a mission in Europe.

Shortly after the work was begun there, Mr. Andrews

wrote to his old friends, Mr. and Mrs. White, and told them of the great need for money to carry on the work that must be done. They were eager to help, but they had very little money of their own to give. The people who had money did not feel that they wanted to send it away across the ocean to help people they did not even know.

Soon after this, Mrs. White was given a beautiful silk dress. As she looked at the lovely dress and thought of the amount of money it must have cost, she thought of Elder Andrews and of the need in Europe.

"I cannot use this expensive dress for myself when the mission so much needs money," she thought. "I will use this gift in such a way that the one who so generously gave it to me will also have a reward and a treasure in heaven."

She went to the store and asked the merchant to sell it for all he could get, since the money was to be used to carry the message of God to a foreign land. The merchant soon sold the dress for fifty dollars and sent the money to Mrs. White.

This money was sent at once to the mission of Europe. When others heard what Mrs. White had done, they donated larger sums. More and more was given until Mr. Andrews wrote that the sum needed came at the right time. With what gratitude this brave missionary gave thanks to God.

The Little Lights of God

It was a solemn time in the White home. Many of the workers had been invited to come together at Battle Creek for some important meetings. Now when the time had come for these special meetings, and the ministers and church leaders were all gathered there for the meetings, Mrs. White was ill.

There was an epidemic of influenza sweeping through the country in December, 1874, and one member after another of the White family had become sick. Mrs. White tenderly nursed each one back to health, but now, worn out with her work, she herself lay gravely ill.

Mr. White felt that he could not endure to have all these workers be disappointed and not hear the messages of God delivered to them by His messenger, Mrs. White. He decided to call in some of the elders of the church and have special prayer for her recovery.

What a solemn occasion that was! The sick woman was dressed and brought down from her room into the parlor. She was seated in a large armchair and warmly wrapped in blankets.

Mr. Waggoner prayed, and then Mr. Smith offered an earnest petition to God. When Mr. White had finished praying, Mrs. White, in a hoarse voice, began to whisper a prayer. Suddenly her voice became clear and musical, and her ringing cry, "Glory to God!" was heard through the whole house.

The others looked up and saw that she was in vision. Her hands were folded across her breast as she looked earnestly upward. Her mouth was closed, and she did not breathe.

As she looked upward, a troubled look came over her face. She threw aside her blankets and walked back and forth in the room, wringing her hands. "Dark! Dark! All dark! So dark!" she moaned. She was silent for a few moments and then her face grew bright. "A light! A little light!" she exclaimed. "More light! Much light!"

In a few minutes Mrs. White went back and took her seat. She drew a long, deep breath, in a moment another, and then another. Then her breathing became natural. She looked at those about her in the room. Mr. White stepped forward and knelt by her chair, for he knew that after a vision everything looked strange to her.

"Ellen," he said softly to her, "Ellen, you have been in vision."

"Yes," she answered, and her voice sounded far away, as though she were speaking to someone in another room.

"Were you shown many things?" her husband asked.

"Yes," she said.

"Would you like to tell us about them now?" he asked.

"Not now."

Those who gathered to pray for her were dismissed and left the house, and Mrs. White went back to her room.

Mr. White went down to the Review office on business, and was delayed until sundown; then he came hurrying home through the fast-falling snow. He went to the room where Mrs. White was resting.

"Ellen," he said, after greeting her, "there is to be an important meeting this evening. Do you wish to go?"

The Little Lights of God

"Certainly," she answered. When she was ready for the meeting she walked with her husband down through the snow to the meetinghouse. There she spoke to the company of people. They were so glad to have her with them, for they had given up all hope of hearing her there.

Mrs. White had been fully healed in answer to prayer. Her hoarseness was gone, and her voice was strong and clear.

In the meeting the next evening she told the people of the great work Seventh-day Adventists must do. She told of the vision given to her at the time she was healed, and spoke of the work to be done in foreign fields. She said that she had seen in different parts of the world little companies studying the Bible, finding the promises there of Christ's return. She had seen little companies beginning to keep the Sabbath without knowing that there were any other Sabbathkeepers in the world.

She told the workers that Seventh-day Adventists would be sending ministers to these places, and that the work of publishing the truth would be carried on.

"In vision I saw many printing presses running in many foreign lands, printing periodicals, tracts, and books containing truths regarding the sacredness of the Sabbath and the soon coming of Jesus," she said.

"Ellen," said Mr. White, "can you tell us the names of the countries?"

Mrs. White hesitated for a moment. "No," she said, thoughtfully, "I do not know the names. The picture of the places and of the presses is very clear, and if I should ever see them I would recognize them. But I did not hear the names." Then she added, "Oh, yes, I remember one; the angel said, 'Australia.'"

Thus the vision she had had the day before was explained. At first the world was dark, so dark to her, but then she saw the little lights beginning to shine, dimly and few at first, and then brighter and brighter until the whole world was lighted up. The little companies of Sabbathkeepers, the ministers working, the presses printing the word of God—these were the lights.

A few years later Mrs. White did see some of these very presses printing the message of Jesus' soon coming.

An Angel Points the Way

"I HAVE felt impressed for several weeks that I am to go to a new field of labor," said J. N. Loughborough as he stood in meeting. "I have come to this meeting prepared to go wherever the Lord will call me to go."

This was said at the General Conference session held in May, 1868. A man from California had just made a plea that workers be sent to that faraway field to tell the people there of the soon coming of Jesus. In those early days before there were railroads across the country, California seemed a long way off. But many people had been moving to this new and interesting State during the past twenty years.

Now the need of sending workers to this new territory was being considered by the conference. When Mr. Loughborough heard the appeal he felt at once that California was the place to which God was preparing him to go. Mr. Bourdeau stood in another part of the meeting hall and said, "I feel the same. God has also impressed me that I must go to another field of labor."

The ministers voted that this work should be begun at once, and that these two young ministers should start a mission in California. Mr. White appealed to all to help in raising $1,000 to send these missionaries to the Pacific Coast.

In less than two weeks the ministers were in New York

buying a tent and preparing to start on their long journey. Because the railroad across the continent was not completed, the men arranged to go by boat to Central America. There they went overland to the Pacific Ocean, and boarded another boat that carried them to San Francisco.

They planned to pitch their tent at once in that city, but they could not find a suitable place. They prayed that the Lord would guide them in this new mission field and show them the way to take. At once they felt impressed to go north of the city, across the bay, but they did not know just where. The next day a stranger came from Petaluma, a town across the bay, about thirty miles north of San Francisco, in the Sonoma valley. This man invited the ministers to pitch their tent in that town.

"One day I saw a notice in one of the Eastern papers that two ministers were coming to the Pacific Coast with a tent to hold meetings," he said. "The people of our church in Petaluma have sent me to find the men with the tent and to urge them to hold their first meetings in our town." Feeling that God was leading them in this way, Mr. Loughborough and Mr. Bourdeau went with him to Petaluma. He did not then tell the ministers that a few nights before, one of the members of his church dreamed that he saw two men kindling a fire, and then he saw the ministers of Petaluma trying to put that fire out, but they could not. The men kindled five fires that burned with a beautiful bright light. The man who had had the dream told the people of his church that he would know the men he had seen building the fires in his dream if he should ever meet them.

"There they are," exclaimed the man who had dreamed of the five fires, as he saw the two ministers coming. "Those are the identical men I saw in my dream."

The ministers pitched their tent, glad to know that the

Lord was leading them to this place. Many people came to the tent each night to hear the message. Mr. Loughborough wrote back to the leaders in the East and told them of how eager the people were to hear their message. It was not long until there were five Seventh-day Adventist churches in Sonoma valley.

In a few years Mr. and Mrs. White went out to California. They held camp meetings and encouraged the new believers to build churches. Although they had to return to Battle Creek and carry on the work there, during the next few years they made several trips to the West. The railroad across the mountains was now finished, and the trip could be made all the way by train in nine days. The work grew so rapidly that other workers also were brought from the East to California.

At a later time two young ministers held several series of meetings in the tent which Mr. Loughborough had used many years before. One spring they decided to hold a new effort in Cloverdale, a little village north of Petaluma, but Mrs. White was shown that the tent should be pitched in Oakland, where there were many people eager to hear the message.

"We must see the ministers who intended to hold meetings in Cloverdale," she told her husband, "for the tent must not be put up there, but in Oakland." They started at once for Healdsburg with their carriage and team. When they reached Healdsburg they were greatly disappointed to find that the men they wished to see had already gone on to Cloverdale, and they were told that the tent was all loaded at Mr. Bond's place, ready to be moved to Cloverdale the next morning. Although the sun was setting behind the wooded hills, they felt that they must journey on.

"Let us go as far as the home of Mr. Bond," said Mr. White, "and then we can go on from there in the morning."

In order to do this they had to cross the Russian River. It

James White cautiously rode over and back, choosing the safest way across.

An Angel Points the Way

was past nine o'clock when they reached the river, but Mr. White had no thought of turning back. It was not safe to cross except at certain places, and Mr. White dared not drive his team into the water until he had found where they could cross safely. The river ran swiftly, and it was dark under the overhanging trees. Mrs. White stood on the bank holding one horse while her husband rode the other one through the river. He cautiously rode over and back, choosing the safest way across, and then returned and hitched the horses to the carriage again and drove through the water to the other side, feeling deeply thankful that they had crossed the river in safety. When they rode up the bank on the other side, to their amazement they saw stretching to the right and to the left before them a broad, rapidly flowing river. They had crossed only a branch of the main stream.

They lifted their hearts to God for help, because they still felt they must go on. Again the horses were unhitched and Mr. White mounted one and rode across the stream. The water came up on the sides of the horse, but he reached the other side before turning back. Twice again he rode back and forth.

"Mark the course I take by the mountain on the other side," he called across to Mrs. White. Although she was having troubles of her own holding the restless horse, who wished to follow his mate, she tried to see the way her husband was going in the darkness.

Again the horses were hitched to the carriage and they drove into the river. The water came into the body of the carriage, but the horses went steadily onward until they came out on the opposite bank. From there it was not far to the home where they planned to spend the night.

"Why, if this is not Mr. White," was the hearty greeting that fell on the ears of the tired travelers when they knocked

His Messenger

at the door. The next morning they saw the tent all loaded ready to be taken to Cloverdale. They arranged to have it sent back for use in Oakland. Then Mr. Bond hitched his fresh, strong team to the carriage, and went with Mr. and Mrs. White to Cloverdale.

In Cloverdale they found one of the ministers. He said to Mrs. White, "After looking around, we have decided that the prospects are not good for a meeting here. We feel we should go somewhere else."

This was just what Mr. and Mrs. White had come to tell them. The whole company were soon on their way back to Healdsburg, and plans were laid for the meetings to be held in Oakland, California. These were very successful, and many people learned of Jesus' soon coming. Mr. and Mrs. White now made their home in Oakland, that they might help with the tent meetings. Soon after the tent was pitched and the meetings were begun, Mr. White started publishing the *Signs of the Times* in Oakland.

That summer Mrs. White felt that she should go back to the Eastern States and attend the camp meetings. She wanted to present to the people there the work that was being done on the Pacific Coast. She wanted to ask their support for the *Signs of the Times* that had just been started. But Mr. White was not very well, and he must take care of the new paper, and she did not like to leave him.

"Will you let me go to Battle Creek to try to raise some money for the work here?" she asked her husband.

"How can you go?" he said, as he thought of the camp meeting to be held in California and of the articles that must be written for the papers. "I am overwhelmed with the responsibility. I cannot let you go."

"God will take care of you," she answered simply.

While they were considering what should be done, one

An Angel Points the Way

of the workers, John I. Tay, visited them. They told him of their burdens, and together they all knelt to pray for God's guidance. While they were praying, the Spirit of God filled the room, and it seemed to Mrs. White that she saw an angel pointing across the Rocky Mountains to the churches in the East.

Mr. Tay rose from his knees. His face was white. "I saw an angel pointing across the Rocky Mountains," he said, as he turned to Mr. White.

"Well, Ellen," Mr. White spoke quietly, "I shall have to let you go."

Mrs. White did not wait for another word. She hurried to her kitchen and put a few graham gems and some fruit into a basket for her lunch, packed a few clothes, and hastened to the train. She went alone on this trip back across the Rocky Mountains and the plains, a journey that took eight days.

She went to the different camp meetings and bore her testimony. Everywhere she went, she asked for money to help in the work in California, and she was not disappointed, for the liberal people gave all they could.

At a camp meeting in Newton, Iowa, the people had pledged $2,000 to help in this work, but when Mrs. White had finished speaking, they asked that they might pledge again, and another thousand dollars was added to the gift.

At times Mr. White was in poor health because he had borne such heavy burdens in the cause of God. Still, while he was near where the other ministers were working, he was always eager to help.

"If we could only find a place in the country where we could be by ourselves," thought Mrs. White. Then one day while she was in the Sonoma valley, she found a small well-wooded place for sale near Healdsburg. On it were several fine springs flowing with clear, cool water.

His Messenger

"This is the place we need," she told the gentleman who had shown her the land. "This is just such a place as will please Mr. White."

Soon they were busy packing and moving. In a few days they were settled in their little home in the mountains. There was a great fireplace in the front room, and there both Mr. and Mrs. White spent many happy days reading and writing. From this little parlor came letters of encouragement and letters of counsel to those for whom God had sent messages. Here the angel of prophecy visited Mrs. White many times and opened up before her the plan of the great work to be carried on.

Sometimes they left their quiet home to go to Oakland to work with the brethren there, and they also attended important meetings nearby.

Through the Golden Gate

"Wouldn't you like to go for a boat ride on San Francisco Bay?" asked Mr. Chittenden, a kind friend, one day. Mrs. White was always busy writing, writing, and he thought a little vacation would do her good.

"Indeed we would," all the family agreed. They were soon ready with a lunch packed and were taken down to the dock to board the sailboat. It was a perfect day on the bay, and they sailed across the quiet waters. Once they drew up to a beach, and the children in the party played in the sand.

"I should like to go out through the Golden Gate, into the Pacific Ocean," said one of the party, "but there is no wind to take us out of the harbor."

"A friend of mine has a tugboat," said another. "He will take us out through the Golden Gate, I am sure."

In a short time they were being towed by the steam tug toward the Gate. When they reached the rocky points that guard the entrance of the bay, the waters became quite rough and the waves rolled in. Two of the young women became seasick, but Mrs. White enjoyed the ride.

"The waves ran high, and we were tossed up and down so very grandly," she wrote to her husband, who was at a conference in Battle Creek. "I was highly elevated in my feelings, but had no words to say to anyone. It was grand.

Mrs. White looked out over the waves, filled with wonder at the power of God, who controls the forces of nature.

Through the Golden Gate

The spray dashed over us, the watchful captain giving his orders, the ready hands to obey. The wind was strong outside of the Golden Gate, and I never enjoyed anything as much in my life."

"Mrs. White looks happy, but she is quiet," said Mr. Chittenden, as they rode along.

Mrs. White only smiled and looked out again over the racing waves. That day she had planned, before the invitation came for a boat ride, to write about Christ walking upon the sea and stilling the tempest. How impressive the scene was now as she saw the power of the great waves. She was filled with awe as she thought of the majesty of God and His works.

"He holds the winds in His hands. He controls the waters," she said to herself. "We are mere specks upon the broad, deep waters of the Pacific; yet angels of heaven are sent to guard this little sailboat as it races over the waves. Oh, the wonderful works of God! So far beyond our understanding! At one glance He beholds the highest heavens and the midst of the sea."

When evening came, the sailboat was towed back through the Golden Gate into the quiet waters of the bay, and there they watched the sun sink into the ocean with glorious colors reflected from the sky and in the waters.

The next morning early Mrs. White went back to her writing. But first she wrote to her husband to share with him the wonderful experience she had had on the ocean.

"How vividly before my mind was the boat with the disciples buffeting the waves," she wrote. "The night was dark and tempestuous. Their Master was absent. The sea was strong, the winds contrary. Had Jesus, their Saviour, been with them, they would have felt safe. All through the long and tedious night they bent to their oars, forcing their way against wind and waves. They were beset with danger and horror. These were strong men accustomed to hardships and peril and not easily intimidated with danger. They had expected to take their Saviour on board the ship at a certain point designated, but how without Him could they even reach that spot? All in vain, the wind was against them.

"The strength of the rowers was exhausted, and yet the merciless storm had not abated, but was lashing the waves into a fury as though to engulf the boat and themselves. Oh, how they longed for Jesus.

"In the hour of their greatest peril, when they had given up all for lost, amid the lightning flashes in the fourth watch of the night, Jesus was revealed to them walking upon the water. Oh, then Jesus had not forgotten them. His watchful eye of tender sympathy and pitying love had watched them all through that fearful storm. In their greatest need He was close by them.

"He had told them where to meet Him. They were doing their utmost to obey Him and take Him on board, but a trial of their faith was necessary. And at the very point when despair was taking the place of hope, when they felt that they were utterly deserted, the eye of the world's Redeemer was watching them with a compassion that is as tender as a mother watching over a suffering child, and this love was infinite.

"The disciples were at first affrighted, but above the roaring of the angry tempest were heard the words the disciples longed most to hear, 'Be of good cheer; it is I; be not afraid.' Their confidence was restored. 'Jesus, it is Jesus' was spoken from one to the other. 'Be not afraid; it is Jesus, the Master.'

"Jesus said to winds and waves, 'Peace, be still.' Can you wonder that I was silent and happy with these grand themes of contemplation? I am glad I went upon the water. I can write better than before."

Overseas

"WE WISH to have Mrs. Ellen G. White visit the missions in Europe. We request that you allow her and her son to come to Europe as soon as it can be arranged." This was the message sent by a conference of the workers held in Switzerland in the spring of 1884.

It was ten years since J. N. Andrews had gone to Europe and made a beginning in our missionary work there. Other missionaries had joined him, and the truth had spread through many countries. The missionaries and workers in the conference there knew that Mrs. White could give them much help if she could come and see their work and know their problems.

That fall the General Conference men decided that Mrs. White and her son, W. C. White, should be asked to visit Europe, to encourage and instruct the workers there.

When Mrs. White was asked to go to Europe, she hardly knew what to do. Three years before this, James White had died in Battle Creek, Michigan. She had much important writing to do, and she felt that she had not the strength to take such a long trip. Then she remembered that her Master had said, "My grace is sufficient for you." "Yes," she thought, "His grace is sufficient for me, and He will give me strength. I will go and give what help I can in this great work."

In August of the next year, Mrs. White, with her secre-

Mrs. White recognized the pressroom and the workmen as those she had seen in vision, and she asked for the other man.

tary, her son, W. C. White, and his wife and their three-year-old daughter, Ella, sailed for Europe. On the trip crossing the Atlantic there was a storm. As Mrs. White lay in her berth looking out through the porthole onto the tossing waves, she thought of the ship's compass. Although the ship was struggling with the waves, tossed by the restless sea, yet the compass kept its position.

"It is doing its work," she thought, "always pointing to the pole, even though the ship is plunging in the waves. My soul must stay upon God, whatever comes, calm waves or stormy sea." Through the fierce storm she rested quietly in her stateroom. "Thou wilt keep him in perfect peace, whose mind is stayed on thee: because he trusteth in thee," she softly repeated to herself.

The boat docked safely, and Mrs. White was soon giving advice to the workers and speaking to the Seventh-day Adventists in London. In two weeks she went on to Basel, Switzerland. Mr. Whitney, the superintendent of the European missions, met the party and took them to the mission headquarters. He was eager to show them the new meeting hall and the printing plant that had recently been built in that city.

"Look at this meeting hall before going upstairs," he said, as they started to go up the steps to the publishing department. Mrs. White went in and looked carefully about the large room.

"It is a good meeting hall. I feel that I have seen this place before," she said.

From there she was taken on to the part of the building where the printing was done. The press was running, and the men were hurrying about their work. Mrs. White walked over to the press.

"I have seen this press before," she said. "This room looks very familiar to me." Soon the two young men who were working in the pressroom came forward, and were introduced to the strangers from America. Mrs. White greeted them, and then said, "Where is the other man?"

"What other one?" Mr. Whitney asked in surprise.

"There is an older man here," Mrs. White answered, "and I have a message for him."

Mr. Whitney then explained that one of the men who worked there was away that day in the city.

More than ten years before this, in the vision given to Mrs. White at Battle Creek at the time she was healed of the influenza, she had seen the printing presses being operated in many foreign countries. And now she was seeing with her eyes what had been shown her long ago by the angel of prophecy.

As soon as she stepped into the pressroom she recognized the press as one she had been shown; she even remembered the men she had seen working in the room, and missed the one who was not there when she entered.

A few months after this she visited Norway, and there she saw in Christiania (now Oslo) another pressroom that had been shown her in the vision at Battle Creek.

Mrs. White and her companions visited France and Italy, and held meetings wherever it was possible. As she visited many places of historical interest she called to mind scenes that had been shown her in vision.

"I have seen this place before," she said to her son, as they stood before a cathedral. In Germany she saw with her own eyes many places that the angel messenger had shown her in connection with the work of Martin Luther.

During one of her journeys she was taken to the valleys where the Waldenses hid during the time of persecution. As she looked out over the quiet valleys and the hills where thousands of faithful ones had given their lives for their Master,

Overseas

she said, "What a scene will these mountains and hills present when Christ, the Life-giver, shall call forth the dead! They will come from the caverns, from dungeons, from deep wells, where their bodies have been buried. They will come forth with the sound of the trumpet and the voice of God at that last great and terrible day of the Lord."

There were few Seventh-day Adventist meetinghouses in Europe at that time, and halls were rented in which the people met. In these halls Mrs. White spoke to the interested believers. Sometimes these people would walk many miles over mountain trails to hear her speak. Her heart was touched as she saw them sitting there on hard wooden benches that had no backs, eagerly listening to every word she said.

These meetings meant much to the people, and Mrs. White was eager to help them all she could. Even after she retired at night, she was still thinking of ways to make her visit a blessing to the people who lived in such ignorance of a loving God.

On New Year's Eve, 1886, she had a beautiful dream. She dreamed that she saw Jesus and that He talked with her. He told Mrs. White that He was ever near as she worked for the people, just as she saw Him near her then. Jesus said that He would always be her helper as she humbly worked, and that she could freely ask Him for the things needed to encourage her as she labored.

In her dream she turned to Jesus and said, "Precious Saviour, give me wisdom that I may ever act wisely and be a blessing to others. I need Thy light and Thy presence to go with me; then I will never feel sad in any trials. I want to be the means of saving souls."

Mrs. White awakened, and was greatly comforted by this beautiful dream to carry on the work for the people of Europe. "The peace of Jesus is in my heart," she wrote, "and the softening, subduing influence of His Spirit has been with me through this first day of the new year. The old year is in the past, and the new year is before us. Day by day the record will go up to God. What history shall I make? Oh, that it may be such a record as I shall not be ashamed to meet in the judgment. I want to have Jesus with me every hour."

For two years Mrs. White and her helpers worked in Europe. "Go forward!" she told the ministers. "As we advance in the opening path of His providence, God will continue to open the way before us. The greater the difficulties to be overcome, the greater will be the victory."

In all the years since this visit the people of Europe have been encouraged by her words of counsel. Her books have been translated into many of the languages and are sold throughout all the countries. The oldest workers tell the younger ones of Mrs. White and of her visit to them. "We have heard her speak," they say; "we have seen her humble, God-fearing life." "Yes," answer the younger people, "and we have her books, and they agree with the Bible, and deepen our love for Jesus. Surely God has sent His message to us by His servant."

Strengthened by His Presence

"CAN you not come to the meetings in the Eastern States? We want you to speak to the people and to help in deciding some important matters," wrote one of the leading workers to Mrs. White. She was busy at her Battle Creek home writing some of the wonderful things God had shown her, but she decided to lay away this work for a few weeks and attend the meetings. She knew that it would be helpful to the many people who would come to these large gatherings to hear the messages God had given to her.

After attending several meetings in other parts of the East, she went to Salamanca, New York. On the way she took cold and was almost ill, but she spoke on Sabbath afternoon to a large group of people, and on Sunday morning she spoke again to the people of the city who met together in the opera house. There was a great crowd of people filling all the seats and the aisles, and crowding around the platform. She spoke to them about the evils of intoxicating drinks, and urged parents to train their children in habits of self-denial so that they would grow up to be men and women able to resist temptation.

After the meeting she was so tired that her secretary urged her to go back to her home. "You must go back to Battle Creek and take treatments," she said. "You are sick, and should not try to work longer."

"Oh, do not give up hope that the Lord will give you strength to help in the meetings," pleaded the ministers. "We need you with us." The poor sick woman hardly knew what to do. The next appointment was in Virginia, and she did not have the strength to travel farther. The next afternoon she spoke to a large audience although she was suffering from severe pain in her ears and head. After the meeting she said, "I must go home to Battle Creek at once. I am ill." She then went to the house where she was staying, to rest.

After slowly climbing the stairs to her room, she knelt to pray. Before she had spoken even one word she felt that the room was filled with fragrance of roses. Looking up to see where the fragrance came from, she saw that the room was flooded with a soft, silvery light. At once her pain and weariness left her. Hope and comfort and peace filled her heart.

Then she lost all consciousness of what was around her, and was shown many things concerning the cause of God in different parts of the world. She was shown what she must do to best help the work. How happy it made her to have the sweet assurance that God was watching over her and caring for her.

That night she lay on her bed, her heart so full of happiness that she could not sleep. Many times she repeated to herself the words of Jacob as he saw angels ascending and descending upon the ladder from heaven, "Surely the Lord is in this place; and I knew it not. This is none other but the house of God, and this is the gate of heaven."

The next morning her son and one of the ministers came to see what Mrs. White had decided. She told them of her experience the evening before and of how the Lord had healed and blessed her. "I am fully decided to go to Virginia according to appointment," she happily said.

For two months after that she went from one meeting to another, speaking in several States, and her health remained

Strengthened by His Presence

good. As soon as she had finished this work, Mrs. White hurried back to Battle Creek and settled down to her writing again. She was eager to write as much as possible, for she felt that writing what the angel showed her was a part of the gift that God had given her.

Soon after the first vision in 1844 the angel of prophecy had commanded Ellen Harmon to write, and in all the years that followed she had continued to write. Even when she was spending much of her time in traveling and speaking, still she used every moment she could to write. Often she rose at three or four o'clock in the morning to write letters of encouragement or letters of reproof that the angel had directed her to write.

"I have been aroused from my sleep with a vivid sense of subjects previously presented to my mind; and I have written, at midnight, letters that have gone across the continent, and, arriving at a crisis, have saved a great disaster to the cause," she once said, while telling of how God sent these messages to her.

Not many years after the angel of prophecy had first spoken to her, Mrs. White had been shown the whole story of the world, from Creation to the coming of Jesus. At a meeting in Lovett's Grove, Ohio, in March, 1858, ten years later, she had been again shown this same great view and told to write it for others to read. During this same vision she had been shown that Satan and his angels would try to hinder the work. But she had also been shown that the angels of God would not leave her alone and that she must trust in God.

The next day after this vision had been given to her, she and her husband talked over the plans for the writing and publishing of the story in a book which would be called *The Great Controversy Between Christ and His Angels and Satan and His Angels.*

His Messenger

The powers of darkness had not been willing to allow this important work to be so easily written. Before Mrs. White had even begun the work of writing this book, she had been suddenly made very ill with a stroke of paralysis. She had not been able to speak, and her whole side had been paralyzed. After prayer had been offered for her, she partially regained the use of her body. It was in this way that Satan had tried to hinder her from writing out what she had seen in the vision.

While so very sick she had begun to write *The Great Controversy.* "At first I could write only one page a day," she said at one time. "After this exertion I would have to rest three days before trying to write again. As I worked, my strength increased until I could write several hours a day."

When James and Ellen White had had an opportunity to be alone, she had read to him what she had written. He had listened very carefully and had often made suggestions to change a word here or there in such a way that the meaning would be made clearer.

In September, 1858, the little book named *Spiritual Gifts —The Great Controversy Between Christ and His Angels and Satan and His Angels* had been ready to send out. In later years Ellen White rewrote this book, adding much material that had been shown her in later visions. This she wrote as her boys were growing up. William White often told of how the whole family would sit around the fireplace at night while his mother or her secretary read what was being written.

"Hour after hour we sat and listened," he would say, "while mother read those inspired stories of Martin Luther and other great Reformers.

"Sometimes she would stop reading and say to her secretary, 'I have written about this more fully elsewhere. Look in my files and see what you can find.'

"Then the secretary would find what mother had written

Strengthened by His Presence

before, and it would be added to the story, making it clearer and more easily understood."

Mrs. White was greatly stirred as she saw the great conflict between Christ and Satan opening up before her.

"As I write upon my book, I feel intensely moved," she wrote to Uriah Smith. "I want to get it out as soon as possible. . . . I have been unable to sleep nights, thinking of the important things to take place. My mind is stirred so deeply I cannot rest. Write! Write! Write! I feel I must and cannot delay."

As she rewrote the book, presenting the story more fully, many of the scenes were shown to her again in vision.

"While writing the manuscript of *The Great Controversy* I was often conscious of the presence of the angels," she wrote, "and many times the scenes about which I was writing were presented to me anew in visions of the night, so that they were fresh and vivid in my mind."

Many, many times Mrs. White had been given a message to a man or a woman who needed help. Some of these personal testimonies were gathered together and published so that this good advice could be read by all. Other letters to churches and many general articles were added. These were published in a set of books called *Testimonies for the Church.*

In these books may be found many wonderful messages that God has sent to His people. Although what was said was often especially for just one man or woman, it was a good message for all who were trying to follow the Saviour.

In telling of the wonderful things God had shown her, Mrs. White also wrote a number of other books and many articles for the *Review and Herald,* the *Signs of the Times,* and *The Youth's Instructor.*

Pioneering in a Faraway Land

"Workers must be sent to distant lands," said S. N. Haskell to the people at the General Conference in 1891. "We must have schools to train our young people in their own land. They must be trained as teachers, colporteurs, and preachers." He had just come back to America from a visit to Australia, and he pleaded especially for a school for that continent.

"Can we not send teachers there and establish a school where the young people may be taught?" he asked. In answer, the people voted to send teachers to Australia to start such a school to train the young men and women of that country to work for their own people.

"Would it not be well for Mrs. Ellen G. White and her son to spend some time in this new field of labor and help establish this new work?" he continued.

"Indeed it would," agreed the other workers. They all thought of the wonderful counsel which she, through God's guidance, had given them, and of the encouragement it had brought to the European field to have her spend two years there.

At once the mission board voted to invite Mrs. Ellen G. White and her son, William C. White, to go with the teachers to Australia and help with the work there.

Pioneering in a Faraway Land

When the steamer *Alameda* sailed out of the Golden Gate in November, 1891, Mrs. White, four of her helpers, and her son were among the passengers. At Honolulu they were joined by Mr. and Mrs. G. B. Starr, who were also being sent to Australia.

"As I contemplate the past year, I am filled with gratitude to God for His preserving care and loving-kindness," wrote Mrs. White on the boat the day before they reached Samoa. It was her sixty-fourth birthday, and she felt thankful to God for the years of service He had allowed her to give.

"We owe everything to Jesus," she continued. "I consecrate myself to His service, to lift Him up before the people, to proclaim His matchless love."

When the party reached Melbourne, they were met and welcomed by G. C. Tenney, the manager of the publishing house. He even vacated his new home and insisted that Mrs. White and her helpers move right in.

How happy Mrs. White was to be welcomed by these new friends in a strange land. She at once began speaking in meetings and visiting the Seventh-day Adventists in that city. When she visited the publishing house she again saw printing presses at work that had been shown to her in vision at the time she was healed in Battle Creek many years before. After a few months it was planned that she and her son should visit New Zealand. But shortly before they were to go, she became ill with rheumatism, and since she could not travel, the trip had to be postponed.

"Now that I cannot travel, I will do what I can to complete the long-promised book on the life of Christ," she said. For ten long months she suffered from this disease. Sometimes she could not even walk a step, or leave her bed. Propped up in bed, she wrote much for *The Desire of Ages*.

"I could not have done all this writing if the Lord had not

strengthened and blessed me in large measure," she wrote to the workers in Battle Creek. "Never once has that right hand failed me. My arm and shoulder have been full of suffering, hard to bear, but the hand has been able to hold the pen and trace the words that have come to me from the Spirit of the Lord.

"I have had a most precious experience, and I testify to my fellow laborers in the cause of God, 'The Lord is good, and greatly to be praised.' "

Although she suffered greatly she was glad for this opportunity to write. All through the years it had been her great desire to write the full story of the life of Christ, of His ministry, His teachings, and of His sacrifice for us. "What a wonderful privilege it is," she thought to herself, "to write of Him and His work."

"I walk with trembling before God," she wrote to O. A. Olsen, the president of the General Conference. "I know not how to speak or trace with pen the large subjects of the atoning sacrifice. I know not how to present subjects in the living power with which they stand before me.

"I tremble for fear lest I shall belittle the great plan of salvation by cheap words. I bow my soul in awe and reverence before God and say, 'Who is sufficient for these things?' "

At another time she wrote, "I cannot endure the intensity of feeling that comes over me as I think of what Christ has suffered in our world. . . . He was bruised for our iniquities, . . . and with His stripes we are healed, if we receive Him by faith as our personal Saviour."

Many times as she awoke in the night and prayed, she felt the near presence of Jesus. "The very room was filled with the light of His divine presence. I have felt that I could welcome suffering if this precious grace was to accompany it," she wrote.

Pioneering in a Faraway Land

When summer came to Australia, Mrs. White began to feel stronger, and she was finally able to go to New Zealand to visit the churches and attend a general meeting that was being planned.

"Let us make it a camp meeting," someone suggested.

"Oh, no," said others. "We could never have a camp meeting and live in tents here. It has not been done. Road builders and logging men live in tent houses."

They shook their heads. "No, living in tents would not be attractive to the better class of people."

But the workers who wanted a camp meeting were not discouraged. As Mrs. White went from church to church, she invited the people to come to the conference to be held at Napier. She hoped that this conference would be a camp meeting, just like the ones that were held back in America.

By her great enthusiasm Mrs. White persuaded the people to try having a camp meeting in New Zealand. Up to the beginning of the meeting there was little promise that more than about thirty people would camp on the grounds. Tents were erected for that many. But when the meeting opened, people came in until there were about sixty wanting tents.

The people were enthusiastic about camp meeting now! "Yes, indeed! It can be done!" the ministers agreed. And plans were laid at once that the next annual conference should be a camp meeting!

"Australia will have a camp meeting," the papers announced the next year. It was to be the first camp meeting to be held in that great continent! The workers made every preparation for this camp. They made thirty-five family tents this time, for they wanted to be sure to have enough, but the orders kept pouring in until they needed more than one hundred tents!

How carefully the workers laid out the camp! Everything

must be just right, for this camp would be seen by many and would represent the gospel as much as the sermons that would be preached.

"We feel that the eye of God is upon all our arrangements," said Mrs. White. "And in the order of our camp we must seek to show forth the praises of His marvelous light."

When camp meeting began, there were five hundred and eleven people camping on the grounds. This little tent city was a marvel of wonders to the people of Melbourne, Australia. Thousands visited it and were astonished and delighted as they saw the clean white tents standing in straight rows, with the furniture neatly arranged within each one.

Physicians, ministers, businessmen, and society women came to see the camp, and many stayed to hear the good sermons. "If we did not live so near, we would hire tents and camp right with you," some of them said.

The little tent city was a marvel of wonders to the people of Melbourne, Australia. Thousands visited it, and many stayed to hear the good sermons.

"Have you seen the tent city?" "Have you been to camp meeting?" was heard everywhere as people stopped to talk on the streets of Melbourne.

The Adventists enjoyed it too. After meetings had been held for one week, everyone voted to stay another week. "It pays to have camp meetings," they all agreed.

During the closing days of the camp meeting it was decided to establish the school out in the country. The teachers from America had been holding a small school in a rented building in town, but now Mrs. White told them that the school should be established out in the country where the young men and women could work out of doors and where the school could have its own farm and gardens.

"The school must be located far out in the country, where we are away from the city," she told the men. At once they began to look for a place.

His Messenger

After hunting for several weeks they found a large piece of wild land, far from the city. Mrs. White felt that this was the place for the school. "But the people around here are so poor, and the land is poor," some of the church members said. "See, some of the land is a great swamp. We do not want to live in such a wild, out-of-the-way place."

"I have been shown that the people here need not be poor if they would try to make their land yield food," she told them. "This land will bear good fruit and grain if it is cared for. There are fine springs and streams of water. The swamp can be drained."

To show that she had faith in this new place, she herself bought a part of the land and moved her family into tents while a house was built. Her home she named Sunnyside. The school was named Avondale. This was an appropriate name, because many streams of water flowed through the property.

With the encouragement Mrs. White gave them, the brethren arranged for buildings to be put up, and school was opened on time. What a blessing this new school was to the young people of Australia. More and more young people came, and some older ones too. They were eager to bear their share of the burdens and help clear the land, set out fruit trees and berry vines, and build houses.

Sometimes all the money would be spent, and still so much more needed to be done. Then when others were becoming discouraged, Mrs. White would turn to her Master and He would supply their needs. Once when they were greatly needing a meetinghouse, she urged them to build a church big enough to hold the people who would be coming as the school grew.

"No, let us build just a small building, and build a bigger one when we need it," said some. "Wait until we have the

Pioneering in a Faraway Land

money, and then build a big church," said others. In the night the Lord spoke to Mrs. White and said, "Arise, and build without delay."

When she told the people the next day that the Lord wanted them to build at once a building big enough to hold those who would come to the school later on, they were willing to obey. "We will take hold of the work and by faith make a beginning," said the leader of the church.

The next night there came from South Africa a letter, and in it was two hundred pounds (nearly $1,000) to help build a meetinghouse. How happy the people were! They had obeyed, and God had blessed them. Before they had even decided to build a church, the money was on a boat being brought to them.

For nine years Mrs. White and her family lived in Australia. Through her, God guided this new school, making it a blessing to the field. Soon missionaries were being sent from it to the islands of the South Seas and were working for their Master throughout the whole continent of Australia. In that wild, out-of-the-way place grew up a large school with fine orchards and gardens. This school, built according to God's plan, has become a model for other schools where workers for God are to be trained.

"You must ask Jesus to give you a heart to do His will. He will hear your prayers and give you a new heart so that you will want to do His will instead

A Message to a Girl

Mrs. ELLEN WHITE loved little children very much. She not only loved her own sons, but she loved other children too, and would often say to their mothers, "Your children are very precious to the Saviour. He loves them more than it is possible for anyone to realize." As she grew older she was happy to have her grandchildren with her. As she watched them about their work and play she understood better than ever how God watches over His children and loves them.

One day she overheard Ella White's mother reading to her about the coming of Jesus in power and great glory. The little five-year-old girl listened carefully. "What!" she asked, "Jesus really coming back to this world again?"

"Yes, my child," answered the mother, "Jesus is coming to take His people to be with Him forever. He will take all those who are doing His will."

"Oh," said the child. "Why didn't you tell me before? When is He coming?"

"We cannot tell just when, but Christ is coming soon."

"O Mother, I want Jesus to take me, but I don't think I am ready to go with Him. I'm afraid I haven't always been a good girl. What shall I do?"

"You must give your heart to Jesus, then you will be willing to give up your own way and do the things that please Him."

His Messenger

"But, Mother, how can I do this? It is hard for me to give up my own way. I am afraid Jesus will come and find me doing the things that I want to do instead of the things that He wants me to do. What shall I do, Mother?"

"You must ask Jesus to give you a heart to do His will. He will hear your prayers and give you a new heart so that you will want to do His will instead of your own."

"When shall I do this? I don't want to wait until I say my prayers tonight; can't we pray right now?"

While Ella's mother knelt to pray with her, the little girl said, "Dear Lord, please change my wicked heart. You know how hard it is for me to give up my own will. Help me, Jesus, for I don't know what to do."

Of course, the Lord heard the little girl's prayer and helped her to be kind and good. He helped her to give up her own will, whenever she remembered to ask Him. How happy it made her grandmother to see that even a very little girl could really understand just what Jesus wants His children to do to be ready for His coming.

One night years afterward this same little girl knelt as usual by her bedside to pray. But this night she was not happy, for it seemed to her that Jesus was far, far away, and that He did not hear her prayer at all. Ella was fourteen years old, but she knew that she was not as careful to do the will of her Saviour now as she once had been.

After a long while she crept into bed, and with tears running down onto her pillow, she said, "O God, I feel all wrong, but I am going to trust You and believe that You love me, and that You will show me what the trouble is and help me to make it right."

The next day she and her little sister Mabel, who was ten, were in the kitchen when they heard Grandma White's carriage drive up to the door. The girls ran happily to meet

A Message to a Girl

her. Mrs. White came in and sat down. She greeted the girls and admired the little twin brothers, who were only seven months old. Then she turned to Ella's mother and said in her sweet, gentle way, "I want Willie to call his family together, for I have something to say to them." She always called her son Willie.

Soon all were seated in the parlor. The girls were each holding one of the little brothers, as they often did during the worship hour. Then grandmother took from her satchel several sheets of paper and began to read.

"I was unable to sleep after eleven o'clock. In the night season I was instructed of God. One stood by me and spoke."

Everyone in the room felt very solemn. The girls stopped amusing the twins and listened closely. They knew who it was that grandma meant when she said, "One stood by me and spoke." They had often heard her speak of the beautiful angel that came to talk with her in vision. They had many times heard her repeat words of warning and instruction that the angel had spoken to her for God's people.

Mrs. White read that the angel was interested in this home. She was bidden to tell the children that they needed more time to read and study the Bible.

"Can it be possible," thought Ella, "that God has sent His angel from heaven with a message just for us?"

As her grandmother read on, she realized that the angel had been sent with a message for them. Mrs. White read that the children did not understand that as a part of their education they should be taught to perform the little duties of life well. All their work should be done so well that it would pass examination at any time.

"The girls must improve in forming orderly habits and in keeping their garments clean and neatly mended," she read to the family.

His Messenger

Ella and Mabel looked at each other. If there was anything these two girls hated to do it was to sit and darn stockings and mend dresses. "God has noticed that I dislike doing these little things," thought Ella.

"His angels are watching to see how they can minister to your family," Mrs. White continued reading, "how they can work with your children that they shall reflect the likeness of Christ in character."

Then Mrs. White looked right at the girls as she read: "In the performance of household duties, careless, neglectful habits are being formed. The habits of disorder now indulged in, unless corrected, will be carried into every phase of life, and the life will be spoiled for true missionary work.

"Let your first work be to see that everything in your own room is put in order, the dirt and dust carefully removed. God is displeased with habits you are forming. Form correct habits even in dress, let your appearance be neat and attractive, for the angels of heaven are taking notice to these things.

"Books are to be laid aside for their proper season, and no more study should occupy the mind than can be attended to without neglecting the household duties.

"In doing your daily duties promptly, neatly, faithfully, you are missionaries. You are bearing witness for Christ. You are showing that the religion of Christ does not make you untidy, coarse, or disrespectful to your parents by failing to heed their counsel and instruction.

"Bible religion will make you kind, thoughtful, faithful. You will not neglect the little things to be done to give a neat, wholesome appearance, even to the kitchen. 'He that is faithful in that which is least is faithful also in much.'"

When Mrs. White had finished reading the long letter, she handed it to her son and said, "This is the message I have been bidden to give you. I counsel you all to take heed to it."

A Message to a Girl

She talked a little while with the family, telling them not to be discouraged, that God loved them and had noticed how self-sacrificing they were. Heavenly angels would be with the children to help them correct their wrong habits.

When her grandmother had gone, Ella sat very still, thinking. She had asked God to help her and to show her what was wrong with her life, and that night His angel had stood by the side of God's messenger, giving counsel and advice. He had even mentioned Ella and Mabel by name.

Ella arose from her chair determined to do her work the very best she could. "Come on, Mabel," she said. The girls went to their own room and began dusting and cleaning. Soon the room was as neat and orderly as any room could be. The books stood straight and even on the bookshelves; clothes closet, bureau drawers, and every corner of the room were thoroughly cleaned.

"The angels saw it all," Ella told Mabel, "but if they noticed when we slighted the work, they will notice too when it is well done."

The house where they lived, in a half-deserted village in Australia, was old and hard to keep clean. The floors were made from rough boards that must be scrubbed with a scrub brush, and there were none of the modern helps that make housekeeping easy. There was no running hot water, no electricity, no washing machine. This made the housework hard to do, and each girl had to do her share.

It was Mabel's task to clean and shine a long row of lamps, and fill them with fresh oil every day.

A little later when the mother came into the kitchen, she found the little girl looking at the row of lamps. "I didn't shine all eleven chimneys," Mabel was saying wistfully, "but I'll try to do them better after this."

"Be patient a little longer," said the mother in her cheery

way. "We'll soon have a nice little home of our own out in the woods near the new school." Then she added, "But in the meantime let us all do our best to make this poor old house as pleasant as possible for one another, and for the angels, who are unselfish enough to leave heaven, where everything is in perfect order, and come down here to stay with us."

For many years Ella was ashamed to have anyone in the family mention how she had been reproved by the angel, but now, since she has a family of grown children, one of them a missionary in Africa, she realizes that the message which helped her when she was a discouraged girl may also help other girls and boys who are tempted to slight their work and to think that no one sees.

The angels see when we do not do our duty, but they also see when we do it well. How wonderful it is that the great Creator, who hangs millions of worlds in space, notices how we perform our little tasks, and that He counts it real missionary work when we do them "promptly, neatly, faithfully," because we love Him.

The Message That Will Not Die

THE work was well started in Australia, and Mrs. Ellen White felt that she should return with her family to America. There was important work to be done in that land. The angel of the Lord had shown her that sanitariums needed to be established in many places, where the sick people could be cared for and taught to care for themselves.

"In the night season many things are passing before me," she wrote. "Many new lines of work must be begun." Soon after her return, she took a trip through the Southern States. "We need schools for the South," she told the ministers. "Medical missionary work must be started in many small centers."

From place to place she went, giving advice about the great work that God had called this people to do. From many places the workers were calling for her to visit the camp meetings and the conferences and give them help in the work. Mrs. White did what traveling she could, but always before her was the great responsibility of writing out God's messages and publishing them in books, in order that all the people could read them.

"I must prepare books," she told the ministers, "and thus give to others the light that the Lord gives me. I do not want to leave an unfinished work."

His Messenger

Mrs. White bought a home near St. Helena, California, and there she settled down with her secretaries and other helpers to do this work. This home, which was called Elmshaven, was in a beautiful valley surrounded by pine-clad hills. Often, when tired of writing, she rode out through the valley and along the mountain roads. In the spring the orchards were in blossom, laying a pink-and-white blanket over her little valley and filling the air with fragrance. In the fall the colored leaves of the grapevines and the fruit trees made the valley look like a great patchwork quilt thrown down between the green hills. Here in this quiet place God gave His faithful servant, who had traveled so far in His service, a home and rest.

"My health is good, and I am able to do much writing," she wrote to an old friend, as she told of this new home. "I thank the Lord for this. I have decided not to attend so many camp meetings, but to give my time to my writing. I greatly desire to write on the life of Solomon, and I desire too to write on the life of Paul and of his work."

This desire was fulfilled, for a little later two books were published. One was *The Acts of the Apostles,* which gives the wonderful story of the apostles and their work. The life of Solomon, and the kings who followed him, is written in the other book, *Prophets and Kings.*

However, the calls for her to travel still came, and occasionally she would leave her writing and visit the churches and attend general meetings.

"The General Conference is to convene in Washington, D.C.," said Mrs. White in the spring of 1909. "I believe I should leave my work here and attend this important meeting. I am eighty-one years old, and I should go back to Washington by the easiest way, but I cannot refuse the calls to visit churches as I travel."

The Message That Will Not Die

She, with her traveling companions, was soon ready to start her journey. She stopped at Loma Linda, Los Angeles, and Paradise Valley in California, and then went on across the Rocky Mountains to College View, Nebraska, to visit the school and the sanitarium near Lincoln. There she spoke to the five hundred students who were in the school.

This trip from California to Washington took four whole weeks, and during the trip she spoke nearly twenty times.

At the General Conference in Washington, D.C., Mrs. White spoke often. "We are carrying forward a mighty work throughout the world," she said. "We must lay hold on God, and seek Him most earnestly for guidance and blessing."

There were many people from foreign countries at this General Conference, and they came in groups to visit and talk with God's messenger. They told her of how the work was progressing in their lands. Mrs. White listened carefully and then gave counsel as to the best way to carry on the work. How happy she was to meet these workers from over the seas!

"I felt very deeply," she said, "when our brethren who had come from foreign fields told me a little of their experiences and of what the Lord is doing in bringing souls to the truth."

One morning during the conference Mrs. White spoke of her confidence in the message that Seventh-day Adventists have for the world. She told of the part she had had in this work ever since she was a girl of seventeen. Standing before the great congregation, she told of how the angel had given her the command to write.

" 'Write out the instruction I give you for the people,' the angel said.

"I answered, 'I cannot write, Lord.'

"Because of the accident which had nearly cost me my life, I had been feeble in health and unable to write, for my hand

"*Brethren and sisters, I commend unto you this Book.*"

trembled so that I was forced after many efforts to give up the attempt to write.

"But one night the angel of the Lord came to my bedside and said to me, 'You must write out the things that I give you.'

"I said, 'I cannot write.'

"Again the command was given, 'Write out the things I give you.'

"I thought I would try, and taking up a lapboard from the table, I began to write, and found that I could trace the words easily. The Lord had wrought a miracle upon me. Since that time I have written thousands of pages, and I continue to write at the age of eighty-one. Through all these years the Lord has been my helper. Angels of God have protected me, guiding me and giving me strength to carry out the instruction of the Lord. Should I doubt the Lord now, and cast aside the evidences of His loving mercy and power? I thank His name that I have been kept from doing this."

It was the last day of the meeting. Mrs. White felt that she might never attend another General Conference. She came to the platform to give a parting message to those who had come to the conference—a message that they could carry with them to encourage them in their work. She spoke of how much she had enjoyed being at the General Conference, that was now closing, and of what a privilege it was for God's people to meet together. She talked of what must yet be done in warning the world and of Satan's efforts to hinder the work. She spoke of the nearness of the coming of Jesus and the need of getting ready to meet Him, and then exclaimed:

"O what a scene of rejoicing it will be when Jesus shall place the victor's crown upon the heads of the redeemed. Never, nevermore will you be led into temptation and sin. You will meet there those whom you have helped. You will see Jesus in His beauty."

Then Mrs. White turned to the pulpit and took from it the Bible that was lying there. She opened it and held it out before her.

"Brethren and sisters," she said in a clear, strong voice that could be heard all over that great congregation, "Brethren and sisters, I commend unto you this Book." She gently closed the Bible and laid it back on the pulpit. Slowly she walked from the platform—she had spoken her last words before this great assembly of Seventh-day Adventists.

Although she never spoke again in a great General Conference assembly, her counsel is still guiding God's followers. God had shown her the work of His people clear through till Jesus should come, and we shall always have His Word to guide us.

"The question is sometimes asked, 'What if Mrs. White should die?'" Mrs. White wrote to the president of the General Conference at one time. "I answer: 'The books that she has written will not die. They are a living witness to what saith the Scripture.' . . . Of myself I could not have brought out the truths in these books, but the Lord has given me the help of His Holy Spirit." "Whether or not my life is spared, my writings will constantly speak, and their work will go forward as long as time shall last."

After the General Conference, Mrs. White went back to Elmshaven, her home in California, to continue her writing. The Lord spoke often with her there, as He had for so many years. Letters of guidance still were sent from her home to the ministers and the people who were trying to serve God.

She was happy and contented in her quiet home. In the large office room on the second floor she spent many happy hours reading, writing, and studying. When weary of writing she often rested in a comfortable chair, looking out over the beautiful valley surrounding her home.

The Message That Will Not Die

On her writing table were kept several of the books she had written. She would often take a book from the table and sit with it in her hands. Sometimes when visitors came in she would be found holding two or three of the books in her lap, as though she really loved them.

"I appreciate these books as I never did before," she would remark. "They are truth, and they are righteousness, and they are an everlasting testimony that God is true."

Many were the visitors that came to talk with Mrs. White during the last few months of her life. She was always glad to visit with them and give them words of encouragement and cheer. The thought that she would not always be here to speak to them did not make her sad.

"I rejoice in the thought that when I can no longer speak to the people, my books will speak for me," she told a visitor one day.

Ellen G. White finished her lifework and fell asleep July 16, 1915, when she was eighty-seven years old. Her last message to the young people was, "Tell our young people that I want my words to encourage them."

"I know in whom I have believed," she whispered to her son, just before she closed her eyes for the last time.

Although her voice does not speak to us today, still her books carry on the great work that she herself laid down. For seventy years the angel of prophecy had carried to Mrs. White the messages of God. And through all those years she never faltered in giving His word to the world. How precious to the Seventh-day Adventist people are the books that His messenger has so faithfully written to guide them home.

Studies From the Writings of Ellen G. White

WOULD you like to know more of what the angel of prophecy told Ellen G. White? You may read in her own writings, yourself, what she was shown. You will find in her books many wonderful things that she has written that you will easily understand and enjoy.

Here are several studies which will help you to find some of these things for yourself. Look up the page in the book that is named in the study, and read the paragraph given.

In counting the paragraphs, start with the first paragraph that *begins* on the page, not with the last of the paragraph that may have run over from the page before. The full paragraph should be read even though it may not be completed on the page referred to.

Of course, there are many more interesting statements, but these are just a few that will help you to start on your study. In *The Comprehensive Index to the Writings of Ellen G. White* you may look up any subject you want and find the references that will direct you to one of the books Ellen G. White has written.

Studies From the Writings of Ellen G. White

WHERE can father and mother and the boys and girls be happy together on Sabbath? *Education,* page 251, paragraph 1, will give you the answer to this important question.

God has written a message for us, and He asks us to read this message, especially on the Sabbath day. *Christ's Object Lessons,* page 24, paragraph 1.

What do you like to do on Sabbath afternoon? *Testimonies,* volume 2, page 584, paragraph 2, gives a good suggestion.

How may we study outdoors? *Education,* page 100, paragraph 3, tells *three* ways. *Education,* page 119, paragraph 2, gives three questions to answer. Can you answer them? Is there more than one answer? *Education,* page 120, paragraph 2, gives an interesting suggestion to follow. To how many things is Christ compared? The lily of the valley is one flower. Can you see why? Try to find others.

Would you like to have a perfect ending to a happy Sabbath day? *Testimonies,* volume 6, page 359, paragraphs 2 and 3, tells you the secret of how you may have this.

THERE is another book besides the Bible that God has given to you. Can you find its name in *Counsels to Parents and Teachers,* page 185, paragraph 1?

Would you like to study your lessons as Jesus did? Here are some of the things He studied: the trees, the shells at the beach, and even the lichens on the stones. *Education,* page 100, last part of paragraph 2.

How can the flowers and trees be teachers? *Patriarchs and Prophets,* page 48, paragraph 3. There is one word that will help you find the answer.

His Messenger

On the petal of the lily is a message for you. Can you read it? *Thoughts From the Mount of Blessing,* page 96, paragraph 1.

The ants and the birds are teachers. What can they, that have never gone to school, teach you? *Education,* page 117, paragraphs 2 and 3. See also *Education,* page 103, paragraph 2.

Did you ever have your feelings hurt until you became discouraged? You can learn from the eagle what to do when you are discouraged. *Education,* page 118, paragraph 2.

The soundless stars speak a message. *Education,* page 115, paragraph 4, tells it. Look at them some night. Do they speak to you?

How would Jesus have me do my work? *Patriarchs and Prophets,* page 574, paragraph 1.

How does the Lord today regard me if I am faithful in my work? The answer is on the same page, in the last paragraph.

Does Jesus want me to speak for Him? How may I know what to say? *Thoughts From the Mount of Blessing,* bottom of page 85 and top of page 86.

Did the child Jesus help in the home? How? *The Desire of Ages,* page 72, paragraph 3. See also *The Desire of Ages,* page 80, paragraph 3.

When Jesus worked in the carpenter shop, how did He learn to handle tools? *The Desire of Ages,* page 72, paragraph 4.

How can I be His helping hand? *Testimonies,* volume 7, page 64, paragraph 2.

What can I do for Him in school? *Messages to Young*

People, page 183, paragraphs 3 and 4. You will find the same thing told in *Testimonies,* volume 7, beginning on page 275, last paragraph.

What responsibilities can your strong young shoulders carry? *Christ's Object Lessons,* page 348, paragraph 1. A little farther on in the chapter boys and girls are called missionaries. Can you find the sentence?

How long must I wait to do God's service at home? May I do it now as well as when I am grown and am a missionary in a foreign land? What did Jesus do? *The Desire of Ages,* page 74, the last paragraph.

Do YOU know what the last message is that Ellen G. White sent to the young people? It is found in *Messages to Young People,* pages 287 to 289. Can you find the statement, "Books that are a blessing to mind and soul are needed"?

There is a reading pledge given by Ellen G. White. Can you find it and make it your pledge? It is found in *Testimonies,* volume 7, page 64.

Another pledge is given in *Testimonies,* volume 5, the last three lines of page 18 and the upper part of page 19.

Are you preparing for God's work? What kind of house cleaning will help you? *Messages to Young People,* page 286.

Did you know that the books you choose from the library tell others about you? *Messages to Young People,* page 273, paragraph 3.

Ellen G. White was shown a scale weighing thoughts and interests. Read the story in *Testimonies,* volume 1, page

His Messenger

124, paragraph 2. Which way would the scales go if your thoughts and books were weighed?

What happens when you read something hastily that you do not care to remember? Read the answer in *The Ministry of Healing,* bottom of page 445 and top of page 446.

Education, page 185, paragraph 1, tells how Jesus developed a good mind. If you study this paragraph carefully you will find two secrets that will help you develop a good mind too.

You are looking for Jesus to come soon. Would you like to know what will happen before He comes? Ellen G. White describes the scenes as the angel showed them to her in vision. You may read this in *Early Writings,* pages 282 to 285, in the chapter entitled "The Time of Trouble."

Now you will want to read of the wonderful deliverance of God's people. That is the next chapter, beginning on page 285 in *Early Writings.* This is one of the most thrilling scenes that was ever shown to God's messenger.

The first vision given to Ellen G. White told of the second coming of Jesus. You will find this in *Testimonies,* volume 1, beginning on page 58, or *Early Writings,* beginning on page 14.

The Great Controversy gives a wonderful description of the coming of Jesus. This vision was shown to Mrs. White several times as she was writing the book. On page 640 of *The Great Controversy,* the middle of the page, begins the story of Jesus' appearing.

Think of the joy that will come to you as you watch your Saviour come. *Early Writings,* page 272, the last paragraph, describes this happiness.

Do you know what is the first thing that will be given you in heaven by Jesus Himself? Read the first paragraph of the article, "The Saints' Reward," in *Early Writings,* page 288.

When Ellen White was shown heaven in vision, did she think it was well worth working for? The story is in *Early Writings,* page 17, paragraphs 2 and 3.

Do YOU want to talk with Jesus all alone? *Thoughts From the Mount of Blessing,* page 84, says that you may.

What is the first step you must take in approaching God? *Thoughts From the Mount of Blessing,* bottom of page 104 and top of page 105.

How much does God love you? Does He want to answer your prayer? *Steps to Christ,* page 94, paragraph 1.

Can God hear your prayer when you just whisper it while you are in the noisy street? *Christ's Object Lessons,* page 174, paragraph 1.

God gives us a key to unlock His storehouse. Can you use the key? *Steps to Christ,* bottom of page 94 and top of page 95.

WOULD you like to govern yourself? In *Education,* page 287, you will find the first lesson that leads to self-government.

You are now deciding the question of your eternal life. Which way will you take? Read *Messages to Young People,* page 332.

His Messenger

Which way does the signpost "Obedience" point? *Prophets and Kings,* page 179, paragraph 2, tells the story of the signpost.

How may a girl help her brothers? This question is answered in *Messages to Young People,* page 326. The same statement is also found in *Testimonies,* volume 3, page 80, last paragraph.

How wonderful it must have been to really be a disciple of Jesus! Can you be a disciple today? *Messages to Young People,* page 333.

There are three things that will decide whether you will be useful in this world. Can you find them in *Messages to Young People,* page 404, last paragraph? The same quotation is found in *The Ministry of Healing,* page 402, the last paragraph.

Do you know you may be a blessing or a curse to your friends? Read *Testimonies,* volume 4, page 655, paragraphs 1 and 2.

Would you like to be the connecting link between someone and Christ? You may be. *The Desire of Ages* tells you this on page 297, paragraph 2, last four lines.

An impression can be made in wax, and it remains. Can your friends make an impression on your mind? *Testimonies,* volume 4, page 587, paragraph 2, answers this question.

Who would build a house of rotten timbers? Would you? If you are sure you would not, read *Testimonies,* volume 4, page 588, paragraph 1.